The Noise

of

Typewriters

Also by Lance Morrow

The Noise
of
Typewriters

Remembering Journalism

Lance Morrow

New York • London

First American edition published in 2023 by Encounter Books,
an activity of Encounter for Culture and Education, Inc.,
a nonprofit, tax-exempt corporation.
Encounter Books website address: www.encounterbooks.com

Manufactured in the United States and printed on
acid-free paper. The paper used in this publication meets
the minimum requirements of ANSI/NISO Z39.48–1992
(R 1997) (*Permanence of Paper*).

FIRST AMERICAN EDITION

LIBRARY OF CONGRESS CATALOGING-IN-PUBLICATION DATA

Names: Morrow, Lance, author.
Title: The noise of typewriters : remembering journalism / Lance Morrow.
Description: First American edition.
New York, New York : Encounter Books, 2023.
Identifiers: LCCN 2022028422 (print) | LCCN 2022028423 (ebook)
ISBN 9781641772280 (hardcover) | ISBN 9781641772297 (ebook)
Subjects: LCSH: Journalism—United States—History—20th century.
Classification: LCC PN4867 .M675 2023 (print) | LCC PN4867 (ebook)
DDC 071/.3—dc23/eng/20220901
LC record available at https://lccn.loc.gov/2022028422
LC ebook record available at https://lccn.loc.gov/2022028423

1 2 3 4 5 6 7 8 9 20 23

For Susan

CONTENTS

INTRODUCTION

I have an afterimage of Clark Gable at the bus station in a trench coat, with his crooked smile, his shabby integrity. That, of course, is from *It Happened One Night* (1934). Frank Capra in his movies in the 1930s created morality plays about American journalism, turning newspaper reporters into Everyman, their consciences an ongoing test of the country's notion of its emotional reflexes and decencies.

It Happened One Night is a masterpiece of emotional allegories: the entire country seen, for example, as a busload of beleaguered and essentially sweet Americans riding north through a terrific rainstorm in the middle of the night—and all of them singing "The Daring Young Man on the Flying Trapeze." There was a runaway heiress in the back of the bus with a handsome newspaper reporter, incognito. To be an American was to be like the daring young man on the flying trapeze. The ineffably American thing was a sweetness, an innocence, a vulnerability.*

Or to be an American was to be like that spunky little wonder of the 1930s, Shirley Temple—who was another allegory of the time: an innocent, unsinkable child making her way through a bad world.

A curious thing: There was, in the drama of journalism, an implication of childishness, of neoteny almost, as if to say that reporters never quite grew up or that journalism itself never quite learned to act like an adult. Editors, it is true, behaved like irascible father figures—that was the part they were assigned to play—but the reporters by inference were irresponsible children, cases, almost, of arrested development: talented, perhaps, but wayward. Henry Luce was extraordinarily tolerant

---

* In the twenty-first century, the American conscience would notice that there were no black people at all aboard the bus—and that fact would set up a ferociously different and opposite narrative line.

of alcoholics on the staff of his magazines (*Time, Fortune, Life,* and others), as if he thought that was the price he had to pay for good writing. Good editing, in Luce's doctrine, emerged from sobriety, rectitude, and sound judgment—his own missionary father's virtues; but he was romantic enough to believe that inspired writing originated in some other part of the brain, in the region of eccentricity, recklessness, even paganism or madness. When he was an adolescent, the great press lord Luce had wanted to be a poet. He wasn't very good at it. He wrote knockoff Masefield (galloping heptameters). I think he remained wistful for all his life about the Byronic possibilities of the world, for which he knew himself to be unfitted.

The picaresque version of journalism in those days proceeded in a sequence of lovable clichés: the hilarities of Ben Hecht and Charles MacArthur's play *The Front Page* or its even funnier movie version, *His Girl Friday,* or, in the British, Fleet Street version, Evelyn Waugh's *Scoop.* (The 1938 novel was a cult favorite of college-boy journalists of my generation who gleefully quoted the line from the *Daily Beast*'s nature columnist: "Feather-footed through the plashy fen passes the questing vole.") In this rendering, journalism was always ridiculous—but endearingly so. The imbecile press magnate, Lord Copper, asks his foreign editor, "What's the capital of Japan? Yokohama, isn't it?" And the foreign editor meekly replies, "Up to a point, Lord Copper."

Those college-boy journalists had an inside joke:

"President Roosevelt, what did you think of *Brideshead Revisited*?"

"I hate Waugh! Eleanor hates Waugh!"

Very funny. The joke called me back to the time, in the summer of 1982, when the Israelis under Ariel Sharon besieged Beirut and shelled the city mercilessly for weeks to try to dislodge the PLO, the Palestinian Liberation Organization. A friend of mine, a *Time* correspondent, told me he survived the bombardment by retreating to the basement of his apartment building and, as the shells rained down, watching episodes of *Brideshead Revisited,* played over and over again on a VCR.

やこ

They were not entirely wrong, the clichés. Journalism was a rascal—a smoker and a drinker—and the life was picaresque: hectic, improvised, although at times as dull as a clerk's. The pay was bad. You were broke half the time, and often hung over. But you were young enough to enjoy the scruffy mystique and a winking intimacy with big shots—with history itself (which, up close, was apt to look like a bit of a fraud). Did it add up to anything? I wondered. Henry Luce insisted that it did, but Henry Luce—with his money and power and the influence of his Presbyterian conscience upon the middle-class American mind—was a Big Picture man. (Luce believed in capitalizing Big Ideas and once sent a memo to his editors encouraging the practice.) He was certain that everything that fell beneath his gaze must mean something important.

People have forgotten Henry Luce. But he is, in some ways, the key to understanding journalism in the twentieth century. His career raised essential questions—about the nature of journalism, about the politics of storytelling, about the morals of power. Luce was a brilliant American success story—and a cautionary tale.

The journalism I am speaking of owed a lot to the atmosphere of the Great Depression, which was a generation before my time but nonetheless lingered on as folklore—a kind of warning and a moral framework: a lifestyle, an aesthetic.

During the Depression, the reporters were mostly New Dealers, while their publishers were overwhelmingly Republicans. Capra framed his stories around Americans' anxiety about whether they are Good; they imagined that if they were not Good, they must be Evil. Or anyway, they must be Pretty Bad. At the same time, it became a complicated lesson of the twentieth century, starting in the 1930s, that when people try to be perfect, they turn into fanatics. That was the story in foreign countries—in Russia, in Germany, around the time of *It Happened One Night*, which got the Oscar for Best Picture in 1934. Could it happen here? Capra liked to show Americans being tempted by an evil genius (often played by Edward Arnold)—a newspaper publisher with a fascist agenda—but, at the end, returning safely to the arms of their sweet democracy, like Dorothy restored to the farm in Kansas. I sometimes think that the leftist tendencies of twenty-first-century media have their origin in the myths of Frank Capra's movies.

There was a certain amount of decaying theology at work in all of this. In time, the country's Calvinism—the founding religion—had settled for democratizing itself as a cult of emotions. Feelings—like money—give the country a least common denominator: a lingua franca in which people in a diverse society might communicate with one another and affirm their humanity and their citizenship as Americans. Now, instead of hard theological thoughts, the country moralized its feelings. Almost from the start, the need to justify the American enterprise had produced an elaborately sentimental self-image. The Frank Capra movies (for example, *Meet John Doe* and *Mr. Smith Goes to Washington*) were a twentieth-century advance in that art—and so were Norman Rockwell's anecdotal paintings, the glowing American allegories that illustrated covers of the *Saturday Evening Post* in the days when it was a great and influential magazine; my father was an editor at the *Post* in those flush times, after the war. The self-confident and sometimes preacherly and overbearing narratives of Henry Luce's *Time* magazine had an immense moral and cultural influence upon Americans. As a child, Luce, a China missionary's son, learned storytelling from the New Testament, from Christ's parables—each of which teaches a moral lesson. Stories in his magazines would similarly instruct. Hotchkiss and then Yale exposed him to the moralizing Greeks and Romans, especially Plutarch, who sought the truth of things in the lives of great men.

In any case, mass-circulation American journalism (especially Luce's) joined American politics and American religion and American movies in the restless project of making and remaking—or, eventually, unmaking—the national myth.

Journalism in the twentieth century proceeded on the assumption that there was such a thing as objective reality. The task of journalism, said Carl Bernstein—who was a companion of my youth, when we were picaresque rascals side by side on the dictation bank at the *Washington Evening Star* back in the mid-1960s—was to obtain "the best available version of the truth." But in the writing and editing, objective reality tended to become subjective reality; facts were well enough, but important facts needed to be evaluated, judged—characterized. Which was the priority of a mythmaker like Luce—the hard facts of the case or the storyteller's interpretation of them, the narrative line? Is journalism inevitably engaged in the working up of myths, whatever its pretensions to objectivity? A journalist needs a disciplined reverence for the facts, because the temptations of storytelling are strong and seductive.

I don't mean that mythmaking is necessarily perfidious; in any case, it is inevitable. It's a problem of storytelling and, so to speak, of entertainment. Where journalism is concerned, as I discovered over the years, the narrative line is not only a chronic problem of ethics but the key to culture itself—and even the glue that holds a society together.

But in the era I am writing about, questions like that were above our pay grade. We took it for granted that there was something called the truth and that it could be discovered. Start at the level of the cop's truth: The victim was either white or black, male or female. The murder weapon was of a certain caliber. Someone had pulled the trigger. Who? I'm talking about hard facts that are beneath the radar of controversy, of politics. Such facts did not invite abstract speculation. Woodward and Bernstein approached Watergate as a crime story, not a political one; they would knock on doors like police detectives and find things out. Woodward and Bernstein were like the boy in the story of the emperor's new clothes. In *Citizen Kane*, that great fable of journalism and American truth, an obscure clue like "Rosebud" might mean something. Find out what he meant by that, the editor told his boys in the smoky projection room at the start of the movie.

In the twenty-first century, on the other hand, journalism would find itself plunged into the metaverse. Politics and culture would migrate into the country of myth, with its hallucinations and hysterias—the floating world of a trillion screens. There might come to be no agreed reality at all.

⌀

You did not dignify journalism by referring to it as "journalism" (a word that is even now a little too grand, too self-important) unless you put the word "yellow" in front of it. You called yourself a reporter or a newspaperman. News ceases to be news the minute that people know about it. Newspapers were for wrapping the fish or swatting the dog or else announcing, in big, black headlines, a sudden turn in the movie's plot (KANE CAUGHT IN LOVE NEST). The journalist and historian Eric Alterman went overboard in order to make the point: "Reporting was seen as a job for winos, perverts, and those without sufficient imagination to become gangsters."

Contempt for reporters had a long history. General William Tecumseh Sherman hated them (and he had reason, for they sometimes made things up or, worse, they aided the enemy by publishing entirely accurate information about his army's movements), and one day when he learned that Confederate guns had sunk a barge-load of Yankee reporters in the Mississippi River near Vicksburg, he laughed and cheered. The journalists swam ashore and survived, but at least they had gotten their notebooks wet.

When Janet Malcolm died in 2021, obituaries remembered the famous rant with which she opened her 1989 *New Yorker* magazine piece, later to become a book called *The Journalist and the Murderer* (about Jeffrey MacDonald, convicted of killing his wife and daughters, and Joe McGinniss, who wrote a book about the case). "Every journalist who is not too stupid or too full of himself to notice what is going on knows that what he does is morally indefensible," she wrote. "He is a kind of confidence man, preying on people's vanity, ignorance, or loneliness, gaining their trust and betraying them without remorse."

We have all been there at one time or another—gaining the source's trust, smiling, and then betraying that trust. Any reporter, reading Malcolm's rant, experiences a shudder of recognition and shame. But her indictment is too savage, and it belongs to the category of irrelevant generalization. What mattered, ultimately, was not whether you treated a source shabbily but whether you got the story and—who knows—wrote the truth. A (so to speak) secondary betrayal might be the price of getting the story right.

cs

Some journalism earned promotion to the status of literature and, as such, survived. The Library of America collected two volumes of the best Vietnam War reporting—and some of it was splendid and enduring. I think of Joan Didion's essays, some of them still wonderful, years after she wrote them; or of Michael Herr's *Dispatches*, his reporting for *Esquire* from Vietnam. Or of John Hersey's *Hiroshima*, first published in 1946 as the contents of an entire issue of Harold Ross's *New Yorker*. With that book, Hersey achieved a journalistic sainthood that he did not quite deserve. Hersey, also the son of a China missionary, had started out as one of Henry Luce's boys.

I think of some of H.L. Mencken's essays a hundred years ago, which were often as unfair as they were hilarious. When he covered the Scopes "monkey trial" in 1925, Mencken lampooned the entire population of Tennessee as snaggle-toothed and deplorable people, to use the adjective that Hillary Clinton would make famous later on; in truth, most of Tennessee's people were nice enough, some of them nicer and better educated than Mencken himself and, in any case, more polite. The American South, he wrote, in his mode of literary vaudeville, was "the Sahara of the Boz Arts," or "the chigger latitudes." As if the bombastic, lager-swilling, cigar-chomping bourgeois sometime boor and occasional anti-Semite Henry Mencken, who lived with his mother in a row house on Hollins Street in Baltimore, was anything to write home about. At a critical moment, as the country shifted its center of gravity from agricultural and rural to urban—from farm to office, from the harvester to the typewriter—Mencken awakened anxious middle-class Americans to the pleasures of throwing tomatoes at their parents and grandparents, at the places where they'd grown up, and at the churches where their parents worshipped: in Sauk Centre, Minnesota; Spoon River, Illinois; Winesburg, Ohio—to cite the literary points of reference. He taught middle-class Americans to dissociate themselves from—to repudiate—their origins. Mencken was very funny, and I love some of his essays. And he did strike blows for freedom of the press, and some of his targets deserved it; but all the same, he had a bad influence upon the country's manners. Mencken taught his readers to think they were smart—to see themselves as an elite, decisively superior to the ignoramuses they had left behind in the backwaters of American life. The supercilious Mencken strain would become powerful in the twenty-first century's culture wars. He taught bright Americans an idiom of contempt that would come back to haunt the country a hundred years later.

Is it possible that journalism is an art? Mostly, it settled for being a craft. Some of what passes for great journalism in America has had the quality of ranting, for the rant is a characteristic American art form. The news ran adjacent to the funny papers, and those fraternal twins influenced one another: The news stories might be cartoonish and the comics (*Dick Tracy, Little Orphan Annie, Terry and the Pirates*) might borrow ideas from current events.

A cult of feelings, again: The more intemperate the rant, the more entertaining it is, the more the journalism may be esteemed—for the illogical reason that its intemperance speaks of its sincerity, its "passion," as if passionate conviction were the same as truth—and speaks of what the Japanese call *haragei*. Haragei is a samurai virtue that is previous to reason, a sort of ferocious, inarticulate authenticity, which dwells in the hara, the belly of the individual. The belly in Japan is the equivalent of the West's metaphorical heart. (In twenty-first-century America, a principle much like haragei would be sanctified as "my truth," as in the expression "I must speak my truth." My truth is true because it is mine, not because it is true.) In order to prove such authenticity, the Japanese of a former time found it might be necessary to commit hara-kiri. A man considered himself obliged to disembowel himself—displaying the contents of his belly for the world to see—thus showing that he had nothing to hide. Perhaps American journalists and politicians should embrace the custom. It might keep them honest.

A style of American ranting—which is, after all, the national genius—originated with Mark Twain and his brilliant invention, Huckleberry Finn. Huck had an improbably ethical (even noble) mind, a genius for mischief, and a violent, alcoholic father who slept with the pigs, and he told whoppers, which he called "stretchers." He was a representative American character. Twain began as a newspaper reporter out west during the Civil War years. He perfected American humor on the model of "stretchers." Journalism, unless you worked at the *New York Times* in the old days, was often heavy on bombast and fact inflation in the Mark Twain manner: sensational and sentimental, hilarious and squalid—the W.C. Fields touch. Chuck Jones, the great animator who invented Bugs Bunny, the Coyote and Road Runner, Daffy Duck, and other cartoon characters, used to say that he learned everything he knew from Mark Twain.

Academics and moralists were apt to condemn the newspaper trade, the craft (it was, please, not a "profession"), as validation (the intellectuals might have said) of Francis Bacon's line about "mankind's natural but corrupt love of the lie." A lie is so much more entertaining than the truth. The charm of a lie is that you can always make one up; lying is easy, when you get the hang of it. You are not allowed to make up the truth (if you do, it's a lie—or else you are a novelist). Intellectuals (including some who were journalists themselves) dismissed journalism as the illegitimate half brother of decent literature: the Smerdyakov of letters.

&

Most journalism evaporates in a day or a week. In *Scoop*, a veteran hack named Corker tells William Boot, "You've got a lot to learn about journalism. Look at it this way. News is what a chap who doesn't care much about anything wants to read. And it's only news until he's read it. After that, it's dead."

Why bother about it, then, such a shabby, evanescent thing? The answer, I'd say, is that journalism is not, in essence, shabby or evanescent. That's the cartoon version of it. One can have fun with it and tell the war stories and quote Evelyn Waugh; and it's true enough, as far as it goes. But there is more to be said. Journalism touched the history of the twentieth century almost continuously—and sometimes altered it, changing its course from what it might otherwise have been. Journalism became a participant—an active principle of information or misinformation, a sort of adjunct metaphysics that has grown almost infinitely more powerful in the twenty-first century. Henry Luce was one of those who knew instinctively that news doesn't die if you turn it into myth. That was the secret of his immense success and, in some ways, also his greatest flaw.

The mythmaker may be a great truth-teller—or a great liar. The morals of journalism are complex.

Anyway, I'm fond of the subject and the cast of characters. And it was my work. I want to discuss a few representative men and women and to offer a few scenes to give the flavor of the time. And some theories, too, although I don't like theories of journalism.

There's the particle theory of light—and the equally reputable wave theory of light. There is Bertrand Russell's thought that "the universe is all spots and jumps, without coherence or orderliness...it consists of events—short, small, haphazard. Order, unity, and continuity are human inventions just as truly as are catalogues and encyclopedias." Lord Russell thought that people who seek order and unity and all of that have the minds of "governesses." Certainly, Henry Luce had a touch of the governess in his character.

And yet the evanescence—the spottiness, the jumpiness—was not the point. One story naturally yielded to another, but the stories flowed on and on, and the flow was dynamic and continuous. The stories were the country's counter-life or mirror-life, a way of seeing itself—even though half the time it might be as a cartoon or a scandal. Journalism ran along parallel to life or, rather, followed along just behind it, like the car full of gesticulating policemen in slapstick silent movies of a century ago—trying to arrest life, so to speak.

Think of it in another way: The point about the river of Heraclitus is not so much that it is never the same river twice (that's a child's or a pedant's conceit) as that it is always the river, always filled with life and stories—a run of strong, living water. ∎

CHAPTER 1

It was not an accident that *Citizen Kane*, the greatest American movie according to many critics, sought the meaning of the country by telling the life story of a newspaper tycoon, Charles Foster Kane (a character modeled, at least in part, on the publisher William Randolph Hearst, who did everything he could to quash the movie). In some ways, raggedy, onrushing journalism is the characteristic American form—one that captures the provisional, sensational, disjointed, headlong, earnest, and faintly bogus quality of the country's ways. America is an improvisation; so is journalism.

The sled went into the furnace as into a crematorium at the end of *Citizen Kane*, and no one at the time (except for the movie audience, which thought *Aha!*) noticed that the sled had a name; still less did the press or public know that "Rosebud" had a decisive but hieroglyphic meaning. The great personal secret crinkled in the heat and went up in flames. Enigmas in a democracy are sententious; the truth is simple (goes the idea) but hidden from the public eye; the private truth (the lost divinity, the lost innocence, the lost childhood home—the synecdoche of the immolated sled) is even more mysterious than the public and vaguely saturnine enigma of a man like Charles Foster Kane. The truth was always hiding in plain sight; the truth was always getting misplaced. The essential truth was maddeningly inaccessible. And the more deeply inaccessible the truth, the truer it must be—which is true, of course, of God, who is invisible but manifest.

But if that is so, if the true truth of anything is ultimately inaccessible, then what does that make of journalism but a noise and a circus, an enterprise that may be essentially futile? The journalism that was the narrative framework of the movie (*Listen, boys, go and find out what Kane*

meant by the last thing he said before he died—what was it, "Rosebud"?)
failed to come anywhere close to the truth.

Henry Luce, missionary's son, journalist, propagandist for the
American way, and connoisseur of Sunday sermons, became, over the
course of many years, my Charles Foster Kane—an enigma to me, surely,
a man whom I at first disliked and later came to admire and (although I
never met him) even to love. If there is a hero in the essays in this book—
this *causerie*—I suppose it is Henry (Harry) Luce. He is the antihero as
well. That was a curious thing about Luce: He always implied his opposite—a spiritual double, like the Egyptians' ka. There was a good Luce
and a bad Luce. He was bound, for all his life, to people who might be
called anti-Luces—his anti-selves. China and America were anti-selves—
opposites and twins. Heaven and earth were anti-selves. Luce's partner
in founding *Time* magazine, Briton Hadden, was an anti-Luce. Hadden
died very young (of a blood infection in 1929, just before the stock market
crash, before penicillin was available); and presently, the frostily beauteous
Clare Boothe Brokaw became Harry's wife and the principal anti-Luce.
Franklin Roosevelt (at first admired, then despised) was an anti-Luce.
Henry Luce's life was a drama of binaries and anti-selves. It was his anti-
selves that made Luce interesting—that made his mind work and kept it
alert and full of conjecture and longing.

❧

Technically, Rosebud was just the MacGuffin in *Citizen Kane*. I suppose
that the screenwriter, Herman Mankiewicz, and the star and director,
Orson Welles, meant to hint at the sentimental American (and, if you
like, Freudian) point that the truth of the heart is elusive and unexpected
and ultimately unknowable or, anyway, possibly squalid. Then, too, there
was the underlying bromide: American money and success can't really
make you happy. Poor Charlie Kane. He was America—sort of; he stood
for America. But, with all his millions and his power, was he happy? Was
America happy?

That was a typical Harry Luce question. Just after the war, he went
to Paris to see how France was faring. He asked his bureau chief, "Are

the French happy?" The bureau chief, Art White, laughed and said, "Oh, for God's sake, Harry, how can I answer a question like that? There are millions of French people." The anecdote sounded like typical Luce—full of Big Ideas and sweeping generalizations. (One time before the war he sent a note to his assistant: "See me about Hitler.") And yet Luce's was a shrewd question, not silly at all. The French army had capitulated in 1940. The French had lived under German occupation for four years, and many had collaborated with the Nazi regime (while many had joined the Resistance—though not nearly as many as, afterward, claimed to have done so). Many French had done their part in helping the Nazis round up Jews as part of the Final Solution. So, after the war, there was bitterness and much shaving of the heads of women who had taken German lovers. There were trials of collaborators. There was hatred, denial, recrimination. And there was immense relief that the war was over. Luce posed a perfectly intelligent question when he asked Art White, "Are the French happy?"

And what of Harry Luce? Was he happy?

What was the moral of the story of *Citizen Kane*? That everything private and meaningful vanishes while, on the public plane, the country is busy entertaining and astonishing itself with its big excitements and ballyhoo and tremendous lies. The treatment of journalism in *Citizen Kane* is not, to say the least, reverent. The Kane (Hearst) newspapers are sensational and gaudy to the point of burlesque. Orson Welles set up the newsreel sequence at the start of the movie as a parody of Luce's "March of Time" documentaries. Even then, Luce and his media had embedded themselves in American culture, so that the sly Welles could have fun with Luce's self-important resonances (the sonorous, doomy, Voice of God voiceover, for example).

Ulysses Grant was never more American than when he defined history as "one goddamned thing after another." That, in essence, was what American journalism was about. It had the task of reporting—and trying to understand—one goddamned thing after another. The book of Daniel (12:4) might be inscribed over the front door of every Department of Journalism: "Many shall run to and fro, and knowledge shall be increased." ∎

CHAPTER 2

In an exalted or a Lucean mood, I am capable of thinking that journalism is sacred work. I have even believed, over the years, in a vague theology of journalism—of history and witness. The idea of witness speaks not only of objectivity but also of judgment, of moral evaluation. I got the idea, though I do not like to admit it, from Luce, who prayed on his knees and once asked the woman seated next to him at a Manhattan dinner party, "Do you believe in the resurrection of the body?" (She looked with astonishment into his earnest, glacial eyes.)

Luce's mind was formed by the genteel self-confidence of American elites (his own well-born missionary parents, for example) in the Teddy Roosevelt time. In 1908, while still a professor at Princeton, Woodrow Wilson published a book called *Constitutional Government in the United States*—a classic argument for seeing the Constitution and the government it created as a living and changing thing, a drama, an evolution, a progression. "The life of the law...has been experience," wrote Oliver Wendell Holmes. At the heart of Luce's idea of journalism was just that notion of living experience—the sanctity of facts, justly interpreted. One of Luce's great contributions to American journalism was the idea that everything in life (even the most recondite theories of science in the age of Einstein or the most elaborate or scandalous conceits of Modernism or, indeed, the spectacle of the old empires dying, one after another—Chinese, Ottoman, Austro-Hungarian, Russian, British) could be observed, reported upon, understood. The news could be sorted out, coped with, grasped, and interpreted for the great American middle class that would, if all went well, inherit the earth.

Time: The Weekly Newsmagazine had its departments—National Affairs, International, Business, Science, Medicine, Education, Law,

Press, Art, Theater, Cinema, Books, and so on: Luce expanded American journalism's idea of what was news. His magazine's taxonomy produced in its readers' minds an illusion of being, each week, week after week, a comprehensive version of what was going on in the world. All over America, people set aside one evening a week (Wednesday or Thursday, perhaps, whichever day the magazine arrived in the mailbox) to read *Time* from cover to cover. It was a ritual and an entertainment and, to many, a kind of civic duty. *Time's* tone, its attitude, persuaded its readers that the world was as the magazine said it was.

The Luce magazines, especially *Time*, worked on a principle—a psychology—of continuity: A regular flow of magazines (fifty-two of them every year, year after year), a river of narrative, lent a sense of sequence, coherence, and historical logic to a discontinuous world. So much for Lord Russell's "spots and jumps." *Time's* outpouring of facts and knowing explanations told the reader that the world made sense; even when there came immense unexpected events (Pearl Harbor, say, or Franklin Roosevelt's death, or Hiroshima—interruptions of the regular order of things, "the fecundity of the unexpected," as the proto-anarchist Pierre-Joseph Proudhon called it in the previous century), *Time* would still be there in the mailbox to tell Americans what it all meant. Harry Luce's father, the Reverend Henry Winters Luce, died in Pennsylvania on the day of Pearl Harbor (a Sunday), and Luce delayed his grieving so that he might rush into the office from Connecticut and put out a special issue of *Time*.

Americans traveling abroad—even people who were not normally readers of *Time*—spoke of how much they relied on the magazine to keep themselves informed when they were in foreign lands where they had no other regular media. Those travelers pored over *Time*, cover to cover, as thoroughly as the faithful reader in his living room in Des Moines.

Luce's magazines, especially *Time*, worked at creating a sense of fit moral order—an American, Lucean gloss on the world. The implication was that (contrary to everything that the twentieth century claimed about the incoherence of the universe) the mind of God is not discontinuous, that the mind of God is readable and has its purposes even when they may be hidden. "A mighty maze," as Alexander Pope wrote in Henry Adams's favorite century, the eighteenth, "but not without a plan."

Luce undertook to present to his readers a thinking albeit corporate mind, an institutional narrative that spoke in the voice of *Time*. That voice was, on a week-to-week basis, considerably more modulated and various and interesting and unbiased than Luce's critics allowed (for they hated Luce's politics), but still, Luce's premise owed much to the model of a minister in a pulpit, through whom the Lord spoke. Or, to consult the pagan side of the idea, *Time* was like Pallas Athena whispering into the ear of Odysseus on the beach—advising the shipwrecked hero what his next move should be. Luce undertook to do the work of the American superego. He thought of himself as America's conscience, ex officio. And he made a great success of that imposture.

കൈ

We spoke of "church and state"—the state being the business side of things and the church the editorial side (somewhat idealized and endowed with a reverence it did not necessarily deserve). Luce was both church and state, because he owned the whole works, and his word on either side of the operation was law; but he kept the two roles separate and would not even permit people from the business side to set foot on the editorial floors.

Luce's example taught me to think of journalism as an essentially (though vaguely) religious undertaking. It's a dangerous and sometimes a foolish premise. But however merely scruffy or sordid, journalism might nonetheless be like the whisky priest in Graham Greene's novel *The Power and the Glory*—a kind of holy sinner. The sacred character of the vocation may travel about in disreputable disguise, even in disgrace. But it still has the power to administer the sacraments.

It used to, anyway. Journalism has become both more respectable and more disreputable since I was young. It has certainly changed—in its purposes and its technology and its metaphysics.

Vladimir Putin made the case for the sacredness of the work of free, independent journalism in his 2022 war against Ukraine. Even in the age of the internet, Putin mostly prevented his own people in Russia from learning the truth of it.

On the other hand, Lord Beaverbrook called it "the black art of journalism," introducing the thought that journalism's work may be diabolical, not sacred. (People thought that little Max Aitken, 1st Baron Beaverbrook, was sort of diabolical himself.) Luce's enemies accused him of practicing a black art; or they said that what he did was not journalism at all. They said he produced something else—mere Republican/capitalist propaganda, news packaged in clever prose nested in slick pages amid ads for Cadillacs and Buicks. They said he was a monster—a master of lies.

It's always been possible to discuss journalism in the lowest and most insulting terms (as sensationalism, trash, filthy lies) or in the most exalted, as when John Milton opened his *Areopagitica* by quoting Euripides: "This is true liberty, when free-born men, having to advise the public, may speak free, which he who can, and will, deserves high praise; who neither can, nor will, may hold his peace: What can be juster in a state than this?"

If there is a metaphysical rationale for journalism, I would formulate it as follows:

Theologians refer to the *creatio continua*: If it is true that we live, moment to moment, in the ongoing Creation—in the rich and suspense-ful unfolding of the All, of all realities and all illusions, of the mind of the universe or whatever it is that we call God—then the journalist has the important work to do: as witness, as Ishmael, charged to report and to understand and, as necessary, to warn the world. The journalist's job is to keep watch over the ongoing Creation. Who else will do it? Politicians? Lawyers? The White House press secretary? ∎

CHAPTER 3

Graham Greene made much of Americans' destructive innocence (naivete, ignorance) in Vietnam. In the middle of the Eisenhower years, he
claimed that Americans' military power, in league with their oblivious
innocence, made them the most dangerous people in the world. Greene's
indictment in his novel *The Quiet American* connected nicely, later on, to
the ending that Stanley Kubrick gave to his 1987 film *Full Metal Jacket*: In
that scene, his marines stride across a smoldering Vietnamese wasteland
in the imperial city of Hue, at the end of the Tet Offensive. In manly
chorus, the marines sing the Mickey Mouse song, the anthem of their
recently expired childhoods—

M. I. C. [pause] K. E. Y. [pause] M. O. U. S. E.!

The scene refers to, among other things, the eerily corrupted innocence, the faux-Satanism of some 1960s rock and roll—that of the Rolling
Stones, for example, and their prancing imp, Mick Jagger. The 1960s
were the seedbed of later miseries and heresies. American teenagers went
into battle listening to such stuff on their cassette players. Michael Herr's
battle reports caught the moral wind shear—sweet American youth
(sweet anyway until the day before yesterday, when they landed at Tan
Son Nhut) riding millions of dollars' worth of helicopters armed with
Gatling guns, the latest toys, and disintegrating (as it were, for sport) the
water buffalo down below, the rice farmers in black pajamas who fled
among the paddies.

The road from innocence passes through a thousand stages of error
and stupidity and often ends not (as hoped) in sanctity but in disaster.
When discussing the work of journalism, it is not wrong, on carefully

selected occasions, to speak in the largest terms: not wrong to speak of theology or metaphysics—or of Good and Evil.

☙

The war correspondent Dexter Filkins of the *New York Times*, later of the *New Yorker*, began his book called *The Forever War* with an account of the battle for Falluja in Iraq in 2004.

The scene was as follows: Filkins lies on a rooftop with a platoon of marines. All hell breaks loose. An Afghan voice howls through a loud-speaker at the top of a minaret, "The Americans are here! The Holy War! The Holy War! Get up and fight for the city of mosques."

> Bullets poured without direction and without end. No one lifted his head.
>
> "This is crazy," one of the marines yelled to his buddy over the noise.
>
> "Yeah," the buddy yelled back, "and we've only taken one house." And then, as if from the depths, came a new sound: violent, menacing and dire. I looked back over my shoulder to where we had come from, into the vacant field at Falluja's northern edge. A group of marines were standing at the foot of a gigantic loudspeaker, the kind used at rock concerts.
>
> It was AC/DC, the Australian heavy metal band, pouring out its unbridled sounds. I recognized the song immediately: "Hells Bells," the band's celebration of satanic power, had come to us on the battle-field. Behind the strains of its guitars, a church bell tolled thirteen times.
>
> > *I'm a rolling thunder, a pouring rain*
> > *I'm comin' on like a hurricane*
> > *My lightning's flashing across the sky*
> > *You're only young but you're gonna die*
>
> The marines raised the volume on the speakers and the sound of gunfire began to recede. Airstrikes were pulverizing the houses

in front of us. In a flash, a building vanished. The voices from the mosques were hysterical in their fury, and they echoed along the city's northern rim.

"*Allahu Akbar!*" cried one of the men in the mosques. "God is great! There is nothing so glorious as to die for God's path, your faith and your country!"

> *I won't take no prisoners, won't spare no lives*
> *Nobody's putting up a fight*
> *I got my bell, I'm gonna take you to hell*
> *I'm gonna get ya, Satan get ya!*

"God is Great!"

The shouting continued until the houses in front of us were obliterated and the firing and the music began to die. ∎

CHAPTER 4

Being there is one of the imperatives of journalism. Or it used to be, before the age of screens, which changed everything. Being there is still a good idea.

The opening passages of Ernest Hemingway's *A Farewell to Arms* taught generations of journalists something about a certain purity of witness (even though it is fiction): detail and sequence in the writing, a dreamlike, cinematic unreeling. Joan Didion applied the lesson in her work—as she unfolded the sequence in which her mind considered and assimilated whatever evolving reality she might have under contemplation. I dare say that Dexter Filkins—a superb reporter whose distinction lies not only, I think, in his courage and presence of mind and observant eye under fire but, crucially, in his gifts as a stylist—learned from the same passage.

That sample of the early Hemingway is a famous run of narrative-as-incantation—a moment of great storytelling clarity, with trancelike repetitions and obsessive use of the word "and." I am moved every time I read it. It's worth quoting:

> In the late summer of that year we lived in a house in a village that looked across the river and the plain to the mountains. In the bed of the river there were pebbles and boulders, dry and white in the sun, and the water was clear and swiftly moving and blue in the channels. Troops went by the house and down the road and the dust they raised powdered the leaves of the trees. The trunks of the trees too were dusty and the leaves fell early that year and we saw the troops marching along the road and the dust rising and leaves, stirred by the

breeze, falling and the soldiers marching and afterward the road bare and white except for the leaves.

The plain was rich with crops; there were many orchards of fruit trees and beyond the plain the mountains were brown and bare. There was fighting in the mountains and at night we could see the flashes from the artillery. In the dark it was like summer lightning, but the nights were cool and there was not the feeling of a storm coming.

Sometimes in the dark we heard the troops marching under the window and guns going past pulled by motor-tractors. There was much traffic at night and many mules on the roads with boxes of ammunition on each side of their pack-saddles and gray motor trucks that carried men, and other trucks with loads covered with canvas that moved slower in the traffic. There were big guns too that passed in the day drawn by tractors, the long barrels of the guns covered with green branches and green leafy branches and vines laid over the tractors. To the north we could look across a valley and see a forest of chestnut trees and behind it another mountain on this side of the river. There was fighting for that mountain too, but it was not successful, and in the fall when the rains came the leaves all fell from the chestnut trees and the branches were bare and the trunks black with rain. The vineyards were thin and bare-branched too and all the country wet and brown and dead with the autumn. There were mists over the river and clouds on the mountain and the trucks splashed mud on the road and the troops were muddy and wet in their capes; their rifles were wet and under their capes the two leather cartridge-boxes on the front of the belts, gray leather boxes heavy with the packs of clips of thin, long 6.5 mm. cartridges, bulged forward under the capes so that the men, passing on the road, marched as though they were six months gone with child.

There were small gray motor cars that passed going very fast; usually there was an officer on the seat with the driver and more officers in the back seat. They splashed more mud than the camions even and if one of the officers in the back was very small and sitting between two generals, he himself so small that you could not see his face but only the top of his cap and his narrow back, and if the car went especially fast it was probably the King. He lived in Udine and came out in this way nearly every day to see how things were going, and things went very badly.

At the start of the winter came the permanent rain and with the rain came the cholera. But it was checked and in the end only seven thousand died of it in the army. ■

CHAPTER 5

I have done nothing memorable in my life, and yet all around me, things have happened. There has been a touch of *Zelig* in it. It's been a newsy life in that sense. Early on, perhaps because both my parents were journalists in Washington, DC, I got the idea that history is a small town.

I've had an inclination to write in a tone of aftermath, of elegy. I don't quite know why—except that mine is what was called the Silent Generation, wedged between the Greatest Generation (my parents') and the baby boom; my sense of aftermath may have emerged from my earliest memories of immense dramas being enacted elsewhere (nothing less than world war, with its gods and monsters—FDR, Churchill, Hitler, Mussolini, Stalin, Marshall, MacArthur, Patton, Eisenhower, and the rest—and its denouement in the form of a mushroom cloud). I've been primarily an essayist rather than a news writer, and the essay is a retrospective form. The unkindest interpretation of such work may have been suggested by the journalist Murray Kempton, who wrote that the job of editorial writers and their kind is to come down out of the hills after the battle to shoot the wounded.

Forty years after the atom bomb, in the city itself, Hiroshima, I interviewed a Japanese woman, almost fifty by then but curiously childlike, with a child's voice, who had been out with a schoolmate a little after 8:00 in the morning when the clear blue sky, in a sudden apocalypse, obliterated her world. She spoke to me, forty years after that day, in precisely the voice of the child she had been on the morning of August 6, 1945. The voice was full of wonder. The bomb stopped time. The word "trauma" did not begin to cover it.

The fox knows many things. But the hedgehog knows one big thing. That first atom bomb—which had the frolicsome nickname "Little Boy"—was the One Big Thing.

In the summer of 1945, when I was a child, a few days after the bomb fell, I saw the big black end-of-the-world headlines in the *Washington Post* and *Evening Star* and *Times Herald*, the papers all strewn about on the living room floor and my parents sitting cross-legged among them, reading (I could see it) with unusual attention. On the other side of the world from that little Japanese girl, I felt, as if through the center of the earth, the vibration of her astonishment.

After I was old enough to think about Hiroshima and to write about it in essays—for *Time*, for example—I asked myself, as everyone did, more and more as the years passed: What did it mean? Was there a hero of the story? Who was the villain? America? Or had we come to a place in history where there would be neither heroes nor villains anymore— the place where the two had become interchangeable? And what was to become of storytelling if you had neither heroes nor villains? Would that be a good thing or a bad thing for journalism?

I thought that Hiroshima was necessary. I also thought it was the start of all the American troubles. Luce thought the Hiroshima bomb had been unnecessary. So did Eisenhower. I've been in lots of arguments about it. ■

CHAPTER 6

I went into newspaper reporting because it was the family business. I started when I was sixteen, working at a job my father arranged for me (he knew the publisher), as a reporter-photographer for the *Danville (PA) News*, a daily paper with a circulation of 7,000 published in a small town on the banks of the Susquehanna River. I did that for two summers while I was in high school. I took my own pictures with a ten-pound Speed Graphic camera that I lugged around to assignments; I learned how to develop the photographic plates in the paper's smelly little darkroom. My hands stank of the chemicals. The *Danville News* went out of business years ago.

During a year I took off between high school and college, I worked as a copyboy and dictation typist at the *Evening Star* in Washington, DC, where I grew up; and I was a cub reporter for the *Buffalo Evening News* for one summer while in college. The city desk editors didn't know what to do with a Harvard boy and so, for fun, they kept sending me out into East Buffalo, where everyone spoke Polish and no one spoke English, and my interviews with people were conducted in gestures and grunts. After graduation, I returned to the *Evening Star* for a year as a reporter.

The *Star* was a sweet, slightly antiquated newspaper, but it had a first-rate staff—some said it was the best afternoon paper in the country. It was owned by two or three cliff-dwelling Washington families that had grown somnolent; something of the nineteenth century lingered in its ways, a touch of Miss Havisham. I think it reached its high-water mark in the Coolidge administration. The *Star*'s civilized Republicanism never quite recovered from Franklin Roosevelt and the New Deal.

Yet Mary McGrory and Haynes Johnson and David Broder wrote for the *Star* and they, among others, made the paper distinguished. The

Star had an old-fashioned clarity—a sense of itself and the rightness of the old journalistic ways. But it was doomed, and its virtues could not save it. It was an afternoon paper in an era when evening television news was expanding; the *Star*'s delivery trucks crept along in rush-hour traffic, struggling to deliver the paper to the ever-spreading Washington suburbs. The *Star*, even when I was there in the Lyndon Johnson time, had a wistful, Chekhovian air. It finally went out of business in 1981, long after I had left. I worked there with my pal Carl Bernstein, who served an apprenticeship at the paper before he wound up at the *Washington Post*, where he became famous. He wrote a book about our days at the *Star*, called *Chasing History*.

Carl started as a copyboy, sixteen years old, in 1960, in the summer of the Kennedy-Nixon presidential race. He was five feet, three inches tall, still growing, with a face full of freckles. He was bored by school—a sort of amateur juvenile delinquent, a drag racer who used a fake ID to buy beer on the weekends. Carl was eager, ready for anything. I arrived at the *Star* a few years later, just out of Harvard. We became friends.

I appear on the dedication page of *Chasing History*. The book is a sweet elegy that conjures a vanished world. I show up here and there in the narrative. Carl and I raised hell together. We borrowed money and bummed cigarettes from each other. We got drunk together. We committed follies that were mostly harmless. Later on, we shared our troubles. Nearly sixty years have passed. We are still good friends.

We were both a little bit in love with Mary McGrory. It was hard not to be in love with Mary, for she was a woman of intelligence and fey charm, a soft Boston accent, a touch of the nun and the spinster that, on second glance, was undercut by a knowing air that was unexpectedly sexy. She had an observant and penetrating way of writing, intensely personal yet coldly objective—subtle and ruthless at the same time. She sat at a desk at the back of the *Evening Star*'s newsroom, near the big windows looking out on Virginia Avenue SE (a view of the freeway, mostly). You found her there in the evenings, when she came in from covering hearings on the Hill or some such business. She worked late, writing her overnight piece—half news story, half opinion piece. She wrote slowly, with a pack of Marlboros on the desk in front of her. She might take five or ten minutes to think through one sentence—even one word. She had no husband or children to go home to. She never married and she never hurried. She was very Irish and close to the Kennedys, but sometimes very rough on them. She could be brutal, unforgiving. She had a fine sense of justice—a hard core of authority underneath the soft manners and the faux dithering with which she sometimes manipulated men and persuaded them to carry her bags from the press bus to the hotel when they were out covering a presidential campaign. She began her career as a columnist in the early 1950s, when the *Star* took her from her post as a book reviewer and assigned her to write about Senator Joseph McCarthy and his Inquisition. She thought of him as the Irish bullyboy she'd met a hundred times at CYO dances when she was a girl in Boston.

Carl and I were on the local, city desk side of the news. Even when he was little more than a child at the *Star*, Carl was a serious student of newspaper work and how it is done. I was not. Carl had immense respect for the work—a sort of awe—and I had little. I was a snob and a little ashamed of the triviality of the stories we had to cover. So many of us wanted to be novelists and poets; newspaper reporting was an initiation, a kind of slumming. (And where was the ex–English major slaving away at the copy desk of the *Toledo Blade* or the *Kansas City Star* who did not wince, as if stabbed, when he remembered W.B. Yeats's line—in his poem "Why Should Not Old Men Be Mad?"—"Some have known a likely lad / that had a sound fly-fisher's wrist / Turn to a drunken journalist.")

The detectives down at police headquarters—who typed their reports slowly, using the hovering forefinger of the right hand only—called me "Hemingway." I drank now and then with the detectives in the homicide squad on Saturday nights, to soften them up and make them inclined to volunteer information (I brought the bottle, and they didn't say no); but when I arrived in the press room at headquarters on Saturday mornings, I carried a copy of the poems of Andrei Voznesenski to pass the time as I half-listened to the police radio droning in the background. You knew the numbers of the police cruisers (Cruisers 20 through 25 were homicide cruisers, for example), so it was possible to read Voznesenski while at the same time being aware of the dispatcher's droning and alert to decode his instructions to the police cars: If he sent Cruiser 24 to such and such an address, you knew you had a murder; whether you got excited about it depended on the address. The *Star* was a white newspaper in a segregated city. A murder in a black neighborhood might, in the course of things, be worth three paragraphs on the inside of the paper. A white murder might go on the front page.

℀

In the movie *Citizen Kane*, the young Charles Foster Kane tells his guardian, Mr. Thatcher, "I think it would be fun to run a newspaper." Sometimes it was also fun to work for a newspaper. But sometimes not.

Haynes Johnson was maddened by the triviality of it all. He and I had desks next to one another in the *Evening Star* newsroom. Haynes was a tall, handsome, quietly charismatic character with very black and intelligent eyes, thinning black hair, and a hoarsely purring voice. We sat there reading the morning papers and drinking bitter coffee from the coffee cart and waiting for an editor on the city desk to holler at one of us to check out a report of a cat in a tree or a warehouse fire or some such tragedy. The morning dragged on. Haynes (who later won a Pulitzer Prize covering civil rights struggles of the 1960s and became recognized as a distinguished journalist, a master of epic subjects like race in America or the political mood of the country in the autumn of a presidential election year) stared straight ahead and, not speaking to me exactly but rather to himself, or to the universe, muttered, over and over, "What the fuck am I doing with my fucking life?"

His father, Malcolm Johnson, had won a Pulitzer Prize for his coverage of racketeering on the New York waterfront for the *New York Sun*—that reporting had been the basis for the Marlon Brando movie *On the Waterfront*. And here was the son, Haynes, wasting his life (as he thought at the time) waiting for a cat to go up a tree and discover that it did not quite know how to climb down.

The *Star* had the old journalistic virtues—its editors were puritanical in their devotion to facts. If you used an adverb or adjective, you had better have a good reason. The word was spelled *adviser*, not *advisor*. It was *supersede*, not *supercede*. Use of the first-person singular was almost a firing offense. It was, in any case, a faux pas; or at best an eccentricity that, if it actually worked in the story, as sometimes but rarely happened, might be grudgingly allowed; there would be a little flurry of surprise and even awe around the city desk when such a stunt got into the paper, as if the wise guy had gotten away with mooning the publisher.

"Journalism" was not the same as media now. The forms and technology were massively different. Journalism meant newspapers mostly. Radio news was a minor presence and television news was just getting started. We regarded TV news reporters with contempt; their work, we thought, was a sort of playacting. When they showed up—at a crime scene, for example—they had no idea what was going on; they preened and looked confused and asked the reporters from the newspapers what was what. We had an entirely misguided confidence that things would always be so.

The newspapers were not national newspapers but local or at best regional publications (Colonel Robert McCormick's *Chicago Tribune*, which, on its front page, called itself "The World's Greatest Newspaper," circulated all over the upper Midwest). There were the wire services: Associated Press, United Press, International News Service (which later merged with UP).

And there were newsmagazines (*Time, Newsweek*, and *U.S. News & World Report*) with national circulations. Just before the triumph of television, this was the age of magazines, which exerted an influence that people today—brought up in an electronic universe—do not understand. *Life*, the *Saturday Evening Post, Look, Collier's, Reader's Digest, Ladies' Home Journal, Vogue*, and other mass-circulation magazines had broad cultural and political importance.

∽

After a year at the *Evening Star*, *Time* invited me to fly up to New York for a job interview, and a few weeks later, I was installed in a small office on the twenty-fifth floor of the Time-Life Building in Rockefeller Center.

My job was writing the magazine's People section. I hated the work, writing gossip items about Richard Burton and Elizabeth Taylor or Sophia Loren or John-John and the widow Kennedy. But—after the almost

Dickensian poverty of the *Evening Star*—I was amazed to find that you could push a button on your desk to summon a copyboy and could hand him an expense advance requisition slip, and presently he would return with an envelope containing $75 in cash.

Starting out, *Time* paid me very badly (something like $7,500 a year) but only because I'd made so little at the *Star* (less than $6,000) that the magazine's moralistic managing editor thought it would be bad for my character to be introduced too abruptly to *Time*'s big money. When, a few months later, I complained to a back-of-the-book editor named Henry Grunwald, who had befriended me, that the pay was too little to live on in New York, he arranged a several-thousand-dollar raise.

Time was a different world—one that was created by Luce in his image and that was still manned (*manned* is the word) by editors he had trained. I stayed there for many years, until after the turn of the century. I had the best years of the magazine, it may be—the best, at least, from the point of view of a writer. As managing editor, Henry Grunwald introduced bylines. He hired *Time*'s gifted art critic Robert Hughes. The magazine's institutional voice became more varied, its opinions subtler. It became possible to write in one's own style.

Grunwald's successor Ray Cave hired the essayist Roger Rosenblatt, who presently produced a deeply moving, 25,000-word cover story called "Children of War," about young people caught up in war zones around the world. For some time in the 1980s, Roger and I shared *Time*'s essay page at the back of the magazine. His style of writing—his way of doing journalism—was something new at *Time*: a supple and intimate flow of thought, something like jazz: whimsical, highly intelligent, surprising. Henry Luce, at his worst, inflicted a sort of bombastic piety upon events. In Rosenblatt's writing, Luce's magazine, now much evolved, offered subtler exercises in journalistic meditation: the news filtered through a playful, complicated, first-class mind. Harry Luce of course was brilliant—but also, sometimes, categorical and humorless. Roger had the advantage—the virtue—of being very funny. ■

CHAPTER 7

There are a thousand ways of telling the truth—and even more ways of lying.

Remembering the past is itself a powerful act that, so to speak, occurs in the present and may have consequences for the future. Think of how the memory of slavery and the slave trade has altered twenty-first-century American politics and changed the country, its culture, and its future.

Judgmental memory—a sort of law court of retrospection. Also, daydreaming. That was Kenkō's method.

Allow me to veer off the path for a moment in order to introduce Kenkō.

Do you know the Japanese literary term *zuihitsu*? It is usually translated into English as "follow the brush." It is—was—a style of writing, the impromptu, associative method of a favorite writer of mine. Yoshida Kenkō was a Buddhist monk in fourteenth-century Japan, a former courtier at Kyoto—officer of the guards at the Imperial Palace—who, either because of an unhappy love affair or because his patron, the emperor Go-Uda, had died, withdrew to a hut in the woods and composed his *Tsurezuregusa*, or "Essays in Idleness." The legend was that he brushed them on scraps of paper and then pasted them to the wall of his hut like wallpaper—a sort of private editorial or op-ed page. After his death, his friends scraped these pieces off the wall and they were eventually published.

Kenkō's *Tsurezuregusa* is an eccentric assemblage—his gemlike thoughts on life, death, weather, manners, aesthetics, nature, drinking, conversational bores, sex, house design, the beauties of understatement and imperfection.

For a monk, he was remarkably worldly; for a former imperial courtier, he was unusually spiritual. He was a fatalist and a crank. He articulated the Japanese aesthetic of beauty as something inherently impermanent. He believed that the moon behind clouds was more beautiful than the full moon on a clear night; a full moon is a little vulgar, he said. He thought that perfection of any kind (in a house or garden, for example) was rather cheap and commonplace; better there should be an ineffable hint of ruin, of the picturesque ravages of time—weeds, storm damage, faded blossoms, regret. Such truths had an elegance, complexity—the poignance of loss. He believed that the world was steadily growing worse. He yearned for a golden age, a Japanese Camelot, when all was becoming and graceful. The yearning itself was his aesthetic; it was this yearning that produced the interesting, wistful sound of his instrument. He worried that "nobody is left who knows the proper manner for hanging a quiver before the house of a man in disgrace with his majesty." He even regretted that no one remembered the proper shape of a torture rack or the correct way to attach a prisoner to it. On the other hand, he said deliberate cruelty is the worst of human offenses. He believed that "the art of governing a country is founded on thrift."

Sometimes Kenkō sounds like the long-ago WASP Mandarin columnist Joseph Alsop, who now and then regretted the passing of the age of spats and who once, in his house in Georgetown, asked my father, "Hughie, would you like to see my incunabula?" Or so my father told the story. He edited the Alsop brothers, Stewart and Joseph, when they wrote for the old *Saturday Evening Post* after the war, and he thought Joe, with his fussiness about wines and his insistence upon poached eggs on anchovy toast for breakfast, was a fit object of wonder and satire. He thought it was hilarious that Joe read Sun Tzu's *Art of War* in the original Mandarin. My father may have made up the story about the incunabula. But if Joe didn't say it, he should have said it. It would have been just like Joe to say it. I suspect that at some point in their conversation, or perhaps on another day, Alsop had referred to "incunabula" and that, savoring the word and its obscurity, my father had dramatized it and dressed it up as a quotation: "Hughie, would you like to see my incunabula?" Storyteller's license, you see.*

The storyteller needs a narrative line. The narrative line—and the hope of a laugh—has a habit of leading writers astray, tempting them to bear false witness.

∽

One morning in the spring of 1940, Clare Boothe Luce, wife of Henry Luce, was asleep in her bed in the Paris Ritz when the man at the front desk telephoned her in great excitement. He said:

"Madame Luce, you must leave the hotel immediately!"

"What are you talking about?"

"The Germans are coming! They are almost here!"

"How do you know?"

"They called and made reservations."

It's a funny story. Clare Luce told many funny stories, some of them true. She must have been the source of that one (one hardly thinks it was the desk clerk). But the story does savor of the slick, Art Deco style of comedy to which she apprenticed herself as a young woman trying to break into New York's upper sets in the 1920s and 1930s. Her play (later a movie) called *The Women* was full of knowing punchlines that sounded like the one about the German invaders calling to make hotel reservations.

Consider the source. Think about the source's motive in telling the story. Clare Luce was highly motivated to be witty and to be thought to be witty. To be safe, you should interview the desk clerk.

Harry Luce divided the world between those who told the truth and those who lied. It was a ruthlessly binary system of judgment. He turned on Franklin Roosevelt around 1935 or 1936 when he decided that the president was a phony and a liar. Something similar happened

---

* *Encyclopaedia Britannica*: "Incunabula, singular incunabulum, books printed during the earliest period of typography—i.e., from the invention of the art of typographic printing in Europe in the 1450s to the end of the 15th century [i.e., January 1501]."

with Clare. Harry discovered that she was a liar, too. The shock of that knowledge destroyed their marriage, except that the marriage went on and on. (This, in any case, was the analysis of Luce's younger son, Peter Paul, who discussed it with me one day in a coffee shop in New Haven.)

Meantime, his enemies thought of Luce himself as a mass-producer of lies.

೫

Whatever the truth about the call from the front desk, Clare Luce left town, and the Germans marched into Paris and stayed for four years. Then they departed, in haste, and by and by, Ernest Hemingway checked into the Ritz. He drank champagne by the case and claimed that he was the one who had evicted the Germans and liberated Paris. He was impersonating a journalist at the time, on contract with *Collier's* magazine. He was not a very good reporter by then; he told too many lies and he drank too much. His third wife, Martha Gellhorn, a fine and resourceful war correspondent, also worked for *Collier's* (he had horned in on her professional territory and she was bitterly angry about it) and, ahead of Ernest, had managed to cover the Normandy invasion by sneaking aboard a hospital ship and locking herself in a toilet until the ship was well out into the English Channel, on the way to France. By that time, Hemingway was sleeping with the London-based *Time* correspondent Mary Welsh, who would become his fourth wife.

There were correspondents everywhere, and half of them seemed to be connected to Luce's magazines.

೫

These digressions, by the way—about Clare and the Germans, about Hemingway and Martha Gellhorn and Mary Welsh—are examples of the style of *zuihitsu*.

Sometimes Kenkō sounds a little like me. Or, rather, I sound like him. I too have retired to the woods—to a farm in upstate New York. I remember the imperial court and its intrigues: political Washington and corporate New York in the old days—the old ways, the old politicians, old autocrats like Henry Luce, the old scandals, the old wars, and the days when we all smoked cigarettes and drank a lot for lunch. Many of Kenkō's opinions—if you allow for the difference between the fourteenth century and the twenty-first—are my own.

I have adapted Kenkō's zuihitsu method—to a degree—because it is the natural form of the essay; it is also the natural form of journalism. Zuihitsu was essentially the method of the father of the modern essay, Michel de Montaigne, with his funny and erudite and discursive mind. Saul Bellow (whose novels amount to a sequence of essays, dramatized and novelized, jazzed up by Chicago gangster talk and ballasted with oddments from the *Encyclopaedia of Religion and Ethics*) was referring to something like zuihitsu when, in a letter to a friend, he said that a writer wants to hop a freight—a train of thought—and ride it as far as it will carry him.

One or two of Kenkō's essays are purely informational. Essay 149 reads, in its entirety: "You should never put the new antlers of a deer to your nose and smell them. They have little insects that crawl into the nose and devour the brain."

Was that a parable? I came to think of certain American political ideas and politicians and media figures as antler bugs. Fanatics and fanaticisms. I have watched them crawl into people's brains and devour them. ∎

CHAPTER 8

You might think of journalism in terms of another parable, that of Dr. Agassiz and his fish. It is as follows:

When a new student applied to study under Harvard's professor of natural history Louis Agassiz (1807–1873), the great man would take down from his shelf a large specimen jar and, from the smelly preservative fluid, extract a dead fish. He would lay it upon a tin plate. He would sit the young man down at a table and place the plate before him and command him:

"Look at your fish."

No instruments were allowed, no tools with which to measure or dissect; not even a pencil. The only instruments were the student's eyes. The eyes are part of the brain.

"Look at your fish."

Agassiz would leave the room.

The student would be confused, disconcerted. Minutes would pass, then an hour. He would peer at the dead fish and in a while would decide he had noticed all that was of interest about it.

In the afternoon Agassiz would reappear and quiz him and then shake his head and tell him that he had seen little or nothing. Agassiz would leave the room, repeating:

"Look at your fish."

This might go on for several days.

Slowly, the student's eyes would open, and he would begin truly seeing the fish—counting the scales, noting symmetries, dynamics of function, sublimities of design, the greatness of its ideas...

The fish would begin to disclose the secrets of the universe...

I wrote in my notebook: "Never be certain that there is no meaning. Never be certain about anything too quickly."

All journalism implies a concealed metaphysics—even a theology: All truth is part of the whole. All is in motion.

Be tolerant of chaos. Be patient. Wait for stillness.

That is Journalism 101, according to me. ∎

CHAPTER 9

Robert Caro's book called *Working* is, I think, the best one that I've read on journalism—or anyway, on journalism considered as a subject like bricklaying or furniture-making or glassblowing. Caro describes how, exactly, it is done—or how it may be done if the writer is Robert Caro and has years and years, a lifetime, in which to do it.

"Truth takes time," Caro warns in the book. Journalists don't have time. Almost by definition, they do their work in haste. Does that mean they cannot really get at the truth? Is it cheating for Caro to take years and years to produce his story?

Journalists have deadlines. Ordinary journalism is like the labor of an artist working at a fresco, painting on wet plaster, hurrying to complete the story before the plaster dries. I learned to write on deadline, smoking cigarettes, banging away at a Royal desk-model manual typewriter (light blue or gray) that was filthy with purple smudges from the carbon paper. Its ribbon was usually a little ragged from the punishment of the keys, and we had to clean out the keys from time to time; when we were off deadline and had nothing better to do, we'd straighten out a paper clip and lean in close over the mouth of the machine and (like a dentist) pick away at the inky gunk that had accumulated in the rounded keys, especially in the *O* and the *B* and the *P* and the *D*.

Caro accomplished a tremendous metaphysical trick. He is the journalist who suspended time. He turned himself into an ideal reporter in what Thucydides called "the country of myth." He set out on a hero's journey. His great deed was to transform journalism into literature. That alchemy became the work of his lifetime.

In Caro's books, the story became, as it were, infinitely expansible. I thought of the Jorge Luis Borges story "Funes the Memorious," about a man who fell from a horse and struck his head and, after that, knew every detail of everything that had ever happened in the world. Caro the Memorious became the metaphysically perfect journalist of certain zones of the twentieth century.

It used to be that people learned best from the example of their heroes. Caro became one of mine. He seemed to me proof of the idea that journalism is the characteristically American thing—the one that responds most faithfully to the dynamics of American life.

He began his tremendous study of Lyndon Johnson and his times in 1976. Forty-three years later—having published four volumes and while working on the fifth, telling of LBJ's presidency and the disaster of Vietnam—he interrupted that labor to offer *Working*, a brief, highly personal handbook. If I were teaching journalism or nonfiction writing, especially the writing of history and biography, I would build a course around his career, with *Working* as my primary text. I would tell my students, "When possible, do what Caro did." He may be all the education that a writer in this line of work requires.

First, choose the right subject. (If you choose the wrong subject for a biography, for example, it might end by destroying you.) Whether one has only a few hours or several decades in which to do the work, Caro's principles are sound.

Read all available books on the subject. Then read all magazine and journal articles. After that, all national newspaper coverage of the subject—then local coverage.

Plunge next into the documents. "Turn every page," as a newspaper editor advised the young Caro long ago. You never know what you might stumble upon. Luck emerges from diligence. In the LBJ Library in Austin, pages from thirty-two million documents awaited turning. Caro and his wife Ina, his research partner, spent years there, turning pages—panning for gold.

Then will come the business of interviewing—a science and acquired instinct. Caro tells stories to suggest how it is best done. He may conduct the interview as a kind of séance: What did you see? What did you hear? The interviewer keeps repeating the questions, until the interview subject—however irritated by the prodding—may break through to the past, recalling things he did not quite know he knew. Details have a way of returning in Proustian elaboration, with all the reluctant specificities—as when Caro brought Sam Houston Johnson, Lyndon's younger brother (by now a reformed drunkard), back to the Johnson ranch in the Hill Country of Texas. Caro placed him at the dining room table where he had sat as a child and, seated behind him in a chair against the wall—like a psychiatrist or a nineteenth-century spiritualist seeking to commune with the dead—coaxed him to recall the bitter fights that Lyndon had had at that table with the star-crossed father whom he eerily resembled in a physical way (tall, rangy, with those enormous Johnson ears) but feared to imitate in his hard luck and failure. Caro has a gift for getting people to summon their ghosts.

"Interviews: Silence is the weapon," Caro writes, under the heading "Tricks of the Trade." A good homicide detective knows about this. Caro cites Georges Simenon's Inspector Maigret and John le Carré's George Smiley, who both understood how to use the tension of silence. Maigret fiddled with his pipe and Smiley polished his eyeglasses with the thick end of his necktie. Caro reports that "when I'm waiting for a person I'm interviewing to break a silence by giving me a piece of information I want, I write 'SU' (for Shut Up!) in my notebook. If anyone were ever to look through my notebooks, they would find a lot of 'SUs' there."

All of this—the sheer reading alone—is endlessly time-consuming. Years go by. Early on, when Caro was writing his first book, *The Power Broker*, about New York City's urban planner Robert Moses, Ina sold their house in order to keep the work going. It takes nerve and luck to build a book-writing career, especially without a regular journalistic or academic job.

Unless the writer possesses a certain inner-directed character, the techniques will take him only so far. The real secret lies in the ancient disciplines: supernatural patience, determination, perseverance. The Caros' labor in tracking people down, in an age before computers and a national phone directory, inspires awe. In doing research on LBJ's college years—at Southwest Texas State Teachers College in San Marcos—Caro sought to run to ground certain stories that, contrary to earlier biographies and articles, Johnson, among other things, stole an election for the student council and "was so unpopular on campus that his nickname was 'Bull' (for 'Bullshit') Johnson." The former students whom Caro located to discuss the stories were vague on details and said that the man who knew everything about it was Vernon Whiteside, who as a student had worked closely with Johnson and even schemed with him. But everyone said Whiteside was dead.

In time, Caro discovered that Whiteside was not dead; he was living in a mobile home, with his wife, in an unidentified locale north of Miami that had "Beach" in its name. The Caros got out maps and started calling every mobile home court in every Florida town or city north of Miami with "Beach" in its name. At last, they found that a Vernon Whiteside had just pulled his mobile home into a court in Highland Beach. Caro went straight to the airport, flew to Tampa, rented a car, drove many miles to the motor court, and knocked on the Whitesides' door. He explained what he was doing and what he wanted from them. Caro and Vernon Whiteside talked for hours, and when Caro left, he had memorable material for a chapter that shed fascinating light on LBJ's early ambition, ruthlessness, and curious amorality. It was another vivid tile in Caro's enormous mosaic of Johnson as idealist, as supreme pragmatist, and, at times, as something like a sociopath.

No one who has read Caro's first LBJ volume, *The Path to Power*, will forget his evocation of the heartbreaking loneliness—the sheer emptiness—of the Texas Hill Country in the time when LBJ grew up there, before the advent of electricity. His protracted description of a Hill Country housewife's life—of what she had to do in the way of hauling water to wash the family's clothes, for example, and then laboring over washtubs with heavy, sodden loads, and then ironing the clothes with a heavy iron heated on a woodstove—is eloquent and exhausting. So committed was Caro to his intuition of the indispensability of the sense of place—the meaning of landscape in the formation of character—that he and Ina moved to a rented house on the edge of the Hill Country and lived there for three years. He slept on the ground in the middle of nowhere in order to feel the emptiness and to think about how it may have formed Johnson's instincts about the world.

Early on, Caro discovered that he was too facile on the typewriter. So, to slow himself down and to teach himself not to write before thinking, he adopted the practice of doing his first several drafts in pencil or pen, in longhand, on long legal pads. With those drafts completed, he would switch to his Smith-Corona electric typewriter, which he still uses. He honors the writing habits of his youth, before the coming of computers, which he never touches. He puts his words on paper. He dresses in jacket and tie when he goes to his writing office, near Columbus Circle. He believes that the formality induces in him a mood to do serious work.

On the typewriter he will write many drafts, and when the galleys arrive from his publisher, he will do still more rewriting. He claims that he would go on rewriting the published book if it were possible.

Caro's central—and teachable—secret is that, if facts matter in the writing of history and biography and journalism, then writing matters, too: that words matter, the aura and attitude of the language, the skill and power of its formulation. Every good writer knows that language is alive—electrical! Caro gives an example in discussing the effect upon him—and on America—of one of the defining songs of the 1960s, "We Shall Overcome." Originally it was "We Will Overcome." The folk singer Pete Seeger changed it to "We Shall Overcome." The meaning changed from being a sort of prediction to becoming a stronger thing, an anthem.

If the dramas of character and ideas in Caro's books have a radiance about them, it is because they are the product of a remarkably integrated mind doing honest work over a long, long haul. ∎

CHAPTER 10

How is journalism to be judged? How do we recognize distinguished journalism? Is it the wonderful writing? (It's often the case, as we know, that it's the liar who has the best prose style.)

Is journalism to be judged only by how accurate it is?

Is it to be judged by its impartiality? Or by its partiality?

By its passionate engagement? Or by its dispassionate objectivity—precisely, by its disengagement?

Great journalism is certainly to be judged by the truth it discloses—but there are many ways of getting at the truth and expressing the truth.

You can tell the truth endlessly to some people and never be believed. In its dreams, good journalism longs for an honest mind at either end of the transaction.

Truth is sometimes scientific, and sometimes not. There is such a thing as constabulary truth, as flat and dispassionate as a police report: Who killed whom, with what? "ADW" in police shorthand is "assault with a deadly weapon." (One morning at police headquarters in Washington, DC, I read on the teletype report that, on the previous evening, a woman had attacked her husband. Her offense was described as "ADW, mop." This was cop humor.)

Sometimes, the truth is inner truth, elusive, psychological, intuitive, difficult—a mood-truth, a kind of neurotic music. Joan Didion was good at that. Her prose sometimes had the haunting quality of the cello. Norman Mailer was good at this, as well—sometimes. His instrument was not the cello. He wrote in a feverish, exuberant way (full of cosmic fancies, bursts of adrenaline); he had alimony and child support to pay (he was married six times and had nine children), and sometimes, as a consequence, his journalism was mere shtick, though shtick with flair. He wrote a great deal of nonsense. I remember seeing him prowling pugnaciously around four or five national political conventions over the years—most memorably at the Democratic convention in Chicago in 1968. That chaotic mess was Mailer's ideal milieu, I suppose—a journalistic mise-en-scène (riot, billy clubs, tear gas, fractured skulls, hysteria, brutality, obscenity, feces flying through the air in brown paper bags) that was worthy of his gifts and inclinations. He liked excess, demonic impulse.

He was a good journalist when he was paying attention, with a shrewd and penetrating eye. But in those days, he liked to drink too much and raise hell and show off and let himself go, in episodes of calculated recklessness—performances. He had an unfailing instinct of self-drama-tization. He was a perfect 1960s man, in his way; he got into the spirit of the thing. He was his own favorite character and the keenest interpreter of himself and his inner ferocities—the journalist as Tasmanian Devil.

Mailer almost legitimized one of the more crooked premises of what, in those days, was called New Journalism (it was hardly new). The idea was as follows: If the writer was not there to see it happen, it did not happen. There were lacunae in Mailer's accounts of events (political conventions, the March on the Pentagon), and you could explain them by the fact that he was absent from the scene because he was sleeping off the excesses of the night before. In the New Journalism, the writer's eye was all—and if the writer's eye was off duty, why, then the record went blank. If you wanted to know about the missing details, you could check the AP's account.

It was performance journalism; the writer's mind was the star of it. There were tremendous effects to be achieved by embracing the idea of history as hallucination, as nightmare even—a visit to the id as to the circus, or to the insane asylum. There were truths to be discovered there, undoubtedly, although they were not the who, what, where, when, why of the Old Journalism that I'd learned in the newsroom of the *Evening Star*. I admired the "gonzo" work of Hunter Thompson because of a principle of freedom (however druggy) that turned his imagination loose and electrified it—the liberation of Wild Turkey and cocaine, or of plain craziness, whatever was available. If he wasn't actually under the influence, he could claim that he was, as I think he often did, because that gave him license; the reader would rejoice or be awed that a man so wasted could write so well.

Tom Wolfe was able to tap into such electricity in his prose, which was also a performance, with special effects (a kind of jazz), but he imposed upon it the discipline of his research, which was painstaking, schooled in the old ways. In this vein, Michael Herr was a hero of mine. He got the Vietnam War, the American side of it, down brilliantly: He immersed himself in it, he suffered it, living among the marines, for example, under fire during the Tet Offensive in early 1968. He risked his life, as they did. He played fascinatingly with the theme of narrative lines because it was hard for the reader to tell—or for Herr himself to tell—who was the hero of the surreal, lethal, heroic/unheroic madness. His prose was full of rock and roll, Sam the Sham and the Pharaohs—and the drugs, the mental music of the American war.

Herr's was immersive journalism of the most harrowing kind. And yet his example reminds me of the disconcerting truth that some of the finest American writing about war is to be found in *The Red Badge of Courage*, written by a man, Stephen Crane, who had never heard a shot fired in anger. Who can explain Crane's deed of conjuration? It is one of the mysteries of American literature—of which the greatest, perhaps, is still *Leaves of Grass*, a work of genius unpredicted by Walt Whitman's earlier work as journalist and editorialist in and around New York.

Being there. Not being there. Later on, I will discuss what was (arguably) the worst piece of journalism in the twentieth century—the work of Walter Duranty, Moscow correspondent of the *New York Times*, whose articles on Stalin at the time of the Great Famine in Ukraine and the North Caucasus won the Pulitzer Prize that year (1932) and stand as the most shaming (and yet fascinating) case of Not Being There—of a journalist who failed to go to the story, even when seven or eight million people were being murdered. Duranty stayed in Moscow and more or less parroted Stalin's line—raison d'état, the Machiavellian dilemmas of power. Malcolm Muggeridge of the *Manchester Guardian*, who had come to Moscow as a dedicated lefty, determined to make his home forever in the Worker's Paradise, smelled a rat the minute he arrived. He headed out to Ukraine and other famine districts to see for himself. He wrote a

scathing series about the famine for the *Guardian*. And yet the reaction
back home in England was comparative crickets. The *Guardian*'s readers did not want to see Stalin criticized. Muggeridge left Moscow and,
somewhat discredited in England, turned to writing fiction.

✌

Joan Didion was a favorite of mine—with her clear eye, her subtle, moody
intelligence.

I first met her one night in the mid-1960s, at a dinner party given by
a fellow writer at *Time*, Keith Johnson, in his Chelsea apartment. Calvin
"Bud" Trillin was there. He'd recently left the staff of *Time* to go to the
New Yorker. Didion was a tiny woman who chain-smoked Camels. She
and her husband, the writer John Gregory Dunne, were visiting from
California, where they now lived. Everyone talked about Hollywood
and movies and how to write them and who was writing what. I was
incredibly green and, having nothing better to add to the conversation,
I interjected, as if it were a fresh and amusing tidbit, that Jack Warner
referred to Hollywood writers as "schmucks with Underwoods." That was,
although I did not seem to be aware of it at the time, the most famous
line about Hollywood writers, a cliché, and there was around the table
half an instant's embarrassment (a flick of glances) that Keith had invited
anyone as stupid or green as I to dinner; and then the conversation flowed
on, and I stayed silent and ashamed of myself for the rest of the evening.

I was not yet used to New York, so different in its ways from
Washington. Journalists in New York thought faster and talked faster and
more wittily than those in the capital, where wit had never been prized
(and may even be regarded as suspect, the sign of an unreliable or insin-
cere mind). Lunch and dinner in Washington were not a performance,
as they were in New York, which had the tradition (or the myth) of the
Algonquin Round Table to set a standard. Table talk among journalists
in New York (as on that night at Keith Johnson's with Didion and the
rest) had an aspect of competition about it. It was sport. The stakes were
high. I was a rube at the table. ∎

CHAPTER 11

I was fond of Abe Rosenthal, who was executive editor of the *New York Times* from 1977 to 1988. He was a volcanic character, ferocious in his perfectionism, brilliance, irascibility. His mind worked at a high pitch of exasperation. A lot of his reporters and editors hated him, or at least feared him, for he was an autocrat, though a splendidly effective one who transformed the *Times*—added many new sections, fired the dead wood, deepened the coverage, the talent. Abe and I became friends during a trip we made to Sarajevo with Elie Wiesel during the civil war between Bosnian Serbs and Bosnian Muslims in the fall of 1992.

Abe had his Lord Copper moments. Not long after Michiko Kakutani, whom I knew at *Time* magazine, was hired by the *Times* in 1979, Abe sent word that he wanted to see her at 4:00 that afternoon. He didn't say why. Michi, a small, intense woman who (like Didion) smoked unfiltered Camels, was the daughter of a Japanese-born mathematics professor at Yale. She'd grown up in New Haven and graduated from Yale. In later years, with more than three decades as a daily book reviewer at the *Times*, she would become, it was said, the most consequential person in the publishing world.

All through the day of Abe's summons, Michi fretted: What could the formidable Rosenthal possibly want to talk to her about? Had she already, in her brief time at the paper, done something to invite his wrath? Was she to be fired before she had even begun her career there? The literary biographer James Atlas, a mutual friend who told me the story, said that she locked herself in the women's room and bit her nails and tore her hair and smoked half a pack of Camels (James was embellishing, of course, as he liked to do) and that by 4:00 she was a nervous wreck.

She appeared at Abe's office.

He motioned her to a chair and began:

"Michi, my wife Shirley and I have decided to grow bonsai trees, and I'd like to ask your advice on how…"

☙

Abe was a loyal friend. Toward the end of Bill Buckley's life—long after Abe had left the paper—the *Times Sunday Magazine* had published an article on Buckley that was accompanied by a full-page, extreme close-up photograph of him that showed every pore and bristling white whisker of his ravaged, unshaven face; running the photo was an act of pure malice, schadenfreude. In the picture, the elegant William F. Buckley Jr. looked like a shipwreck, a bum, like King Lear after a four-day drunk—and the obvious point of printing it was to suggest that his once-stylish conservatism was now, if examined up close, a dissolute ruin. Why Bill agreed to pose for the *Times* photographer I will never know. Vanity, I think. He did not suspect the ambush. He had no idea how awful he would look. He was used to looking handsome and debonaire.

Later, at Bill's eightieth birthday dinner in the ballroom of the Pierre in 2005, I was seated next to Abe. Henry Kissinger sat at Bill and his wife Pat's table. The Whiffenpoofs had come down from New Haven to sing about the tables down at Mory's. Bill read a very long, uncharacteristically tedious speech that (I may be wrong) made no sense at all. Abe and I talked about Elie, about this and that.

And then I mentioned that photograph of Bill. I told Abe how angry I had been about it.

As happens sometimes, a moment's hush had fallen across the ballroom. In that interval, Abe erupted in a voice that could have been heard across the river in Hoboken: "THOSE COCKSUCKERS! THOSE FUCKING COCKSUCKERS!"

He meant the editors of the *Times Sunday Magazine*. Shirley had recently given him a handsome new Malacca walking stick, and now Abe banged it on the ballroom floor until I thought he would smash it. He banged it on the leg of his chair.

Abe was a man of decisive, unfiltered opinions. After retiring as executive editor, he wrote a regular column for the *Times* called On My Mind. My liberal friends sneeringly called it "Out of My Mind."

Abe and his successor as executive editor, Max Frankel, did not like each other. When a friend of mine—John Stacks, who was writing a biography of James Reston—asked Abe what he thought of Frankel's memoir, *The Times of My Life and My Life with The Times*, Abe considered for a moment and then replied with a show of quiet reason:

"You see, John, I am a New Yorker. I am accustomed to dog shit. I know all about dog shit. And when I see dog shit on the sidewalk, I step around it. So there's no need for me to read Max's book." ∎

CHAPTER 12

Thucydides wrote: "Most of the events of the past, through lapse of time, have fought their way, past credence, into the country of myth." He meant: Look immediately at an event, because before long, it will naturally begin to be falsified and pretty soon will have departed so far from its original truth as to become unrecognizable. People will forget or embellish the story and lie to make it a better story, or to bend it to their own purposes, which may include mere self-glorification.

But perhaps it is the other way around. Maybe the passage of time clarifies rather than obscures the truth. Robert Caro thought so.

For surely, Thucydides's famous formula, if strictly applied, would nullify the distinguishing virtue of the human mind—its capacity to reflect upon events, to sort them out, and to learn from experience.

Is it possible that, contrary to Thucydides, it is the present that is actually the "country of myth"—a term with which Thucydides meant to suggest the "country of untruth"? Is it possible that, in the "lapse of time," in the passage of years, the truth of an event becomes more evident, not less?

The first impression—the "first rough draft of history," as Philip Graham called it a few months before he shot himself in 1963—is often wildly wrong. Graham, publisher of the *Washington Post* and *Newsweek*, husband of Katharine Graham, friend of Lyndon Johnson and John Kennedy, had grown increasingly erratic, manic, bipolar toward the end of his life; yet his speech to the *Newsweek* correspondents in London that April had been both eloquent and modest: "So let us today drudge on about our inescapably impossible task of providing every week a first rough draft of a history that will never be completed about a world we can never really understand."

History, both as it is lived and as it is written down, may be understood as an immense weave of storylines and perspectives that have their own hierarchy, different angles of approach. A great mingling of realities. Journalists like Joe and Stewart Alsop did much of their reporting at a high government level. When Joe went to Saigon to check on the war, he often stayed with the American ambassador. Michael Herr and other war correspondents embedded themselves with the grunts. Such reporters were apt to have a truer picture of the war than those who worked at higher altitudes.

Reporters like Jimmy Breslin and Pete Hamill reported mostly on the lives of ordinary people—of cops and working people and petty criminals. They worked the police precincts; they climbed the tenement stairs. That's where they found their stories and their cast of characters. The Alsops—while they knocked on doors of ordinary citizens during presidential election years, honoring journalism's shoe-leather traditions but "big-footing," as the lingo said—spent most of their time interviewing the powerful: policymakers, secretaries of defense and secretaries of state, and generals at the Pentagon, and now and then the man in the White House. Dorothy Thompson became famous covering the rise of Hitler; she and her friend Vincent Sheean were among the first journalists to warn of the Nazis and denounce them. She spent her time with prime ministers and foreign ministers and great authors, and she became a grand dame and a powerful voice in the 1930s and 1940s; she married Sinclair Lewis, the Nobel Prize–winning novelist (a dreadful marriage, it turned out, because of his drinking); she was the model for the Katharine Hepburn character in the 1942 movie *Woman of the Year*. In my father's house there were many mansions—or anyway, there were many different neighborhoods and angles of sight. A great dividing line ran through the heart of journalism—one that separated the powerful from the powerless. It was sometimes as if the reporters had to choose up sides.

ొ

At the same time, the lines run out of the fertile Shinto of the past, through the disorderly present and into the unknowable future.

Journalism has a role—documentary though not dispositive—in getting down that first draft.

Often enough, it gets things wrong. The first impression of the incident in the Gulf of Tonkin in 1964 was that North Vietnamese gunboats had attacked American destroyers in international waters; that supposed attack on the high seas prompted the US Senate's Gulf of Tonkin Resolution, which amounted to blanket permission for Lyndon Johnson to pursue the war in Vietnam in any way he deemed justified. But, in truth, the attack had been chimerical—the result of confusion about misread blips on the destroyers' radar screens. Thus began the American escalation in Vietnam, the fatal plunge into the country's longest war (to date), the first war that it lost.

Four years later, a misimpression of the Tet Offensive (Americans thought the Communists achieved a military victory whereas, in fact, the Communists lost militarily but gained a tremendous psychological triumph) in effect broke the American will to fight the war.

Thus, the essential beginning of what was called "the living room war" (Tonkin)—played out every night for years on American television screens—was, like the essential end of it (Tet), a case of mistaken information or of wrong interpretation of the facts. The war that killed more than 58,000 Americans and who knows how many Vietnamese had a quality of hallucination.

There was the story of the very old man—over a hundred years old—who was brought to St. Petersburg for the celebration of the 300th anniversary of the Romanov dynasty. It was said that as a small child he had witnessed Napoleon's entry into Moscow in 1812. And so, one hundred years later, the czar and the courtiers and the throng gathered to hear his in-person account of that tremendous event.

The old man began, "Napoleon was a very tall man, with a long, white beard."

So much for the eyewitness.

I don't think that I believe that story, any more than Herodotus believed certain whoppers that he repeated about the Scythians or the flying snakes of Arabia or the giant ants of India that mined for gold.

But I like the punchline about Napoleon. ∎

CHAPTER 13

Is it easier to see the truth up close, in the present? Or easier to see it at a distance of years?

This is a variation on the theme of Being There. The distance from the scene of the event created what might be called a zone of fabulation—the space in which a writer (distant in either time or place from the facts) might elaborate his own reality, projecting his own preferences, whimsies, hopes, fears, fancies, interpretations, opinions, or ideologies upon the story at hand.

In China during the 1940s and in Vietnam during the 1960s, there arose iconic disputes between the correspondent on the scene and the editors back in New York. Theodore H. White, *Time*'s man stationed in Chungking, quarreled bitterly with Henry Luce about how Chiang Kai-shek and Mao Tse-tung were to be treated in the magazine's coverage. White had a low opinion of Luce's hero, Chiang—and was a little too starry-eyed about Mao and the Communists. In Vietnam during the early stages of the American involvement, the *New York Times'* David Halberstam and other reporters sent in dispatches deeply skeptical of the Johnson administration's optimistic account. The White House and the Pentagon and the generals in Saigon complained bitterly.

In truth, both the present and the past are "the country of myth." Illusion and truth get mixed up with one another in the refracting dimensions of time—past, present, and future—and (now, in the digital age) in the immense distortions of media, "social" or otherwise.

Bear in mind Ludwig Wittgenstein's question. The first philosophical inquiry that he considered, at the age of eight or nine, was this: "Why should one tell the truth if it's to one's advantage to lie?"

The present teems with error and myth and deliberate lies, which are our daily bread—our consolation, our entertainment, our script and our self-conception, our identities, the stories we tell ourselves. The present may be harder to grasp than the past, for the past at least offers the perspectives of experience, an awareness of what consequences followed from what actions in the past. The Atlantis of my youth—the America of the twentieth century—is easier to grasp than the twenty-first century of my old age, when machines grow more and more precise in their grasp of the universe and human brains become more and more confused—and, paradoxically, more parochial, more hysterical. ∎

CHAPTER 14

A train went off the tracks last night in the Egyptian desert one hundred miles south of Cairo, and five passengers were killed, along with the engineer and fireman.

The report, on the radio, comes to me on my farm in upstate New York and presents to my mind for a moment or two an approximate scene:

I see a train derailed and its cars enjambed and I see the desert stretching away on the margins of the picture, and I take in the data, the numbers of the dead; but they do not come to me as actual bodies, only as numbers.

Who were they?

How did they die?

I think of scenes in T.E. Lawrence's account of the Arab Revolt—his book *Seven Pillars of Wisdom*—scenes in which he and his Arab guerrillas derail Turkish trains in the desert and then machine-gun the troops and even the civilian passengers as they tumble out of the cars.

My imagination goes into business for itself—jumps aboard Saul Bellow's train of thought—and has commenced, by leaps of association, to turn the report of the Egyptian train wreck, with which I started, into a drama that my mind plagiarizes from Lawrence's book from a century ago but which I now visualize by way of David Lean's movie version, which contained a number of such scenes of trains derailed or blown up out among the sands.

News barges in upon the mind of the receiver, which goes to work on its own at recombinations of impressions, scenes, rummaging unbidden through the disorderly inventory of a lifetime to hit upon and gather in whatever stray associations or half-relevant or half-remembered items might in the brain's fast-moving networks of data crowd into the picture—and all of this between sips of coffee on a bright June morning. The exterminator arrived in his panel truck and—while I was thinking about the Egyptian train wreck and T.E. Lawrence—distributed fresh poison in the basement of our old farmhouse. The mice have been living on this farm a lot longer than I have, but I am viceroy here and if the mice don't like it, they can go back to the barn. For a second, I conjure mice spilling out of the house like Turkish soldiers tumbling out of the derailed train.

Words are ghosts, and like all ghosts they have a life of their own— their life in the writing. It is an inventive and ingenious life, after all— viral, as it were, meaning that words throw off pollen and spoor and phantom realities, and that they agitate and proliferate and reproduce and spread and create colonies and universes of their own.

I mention the Egyptian train wreck as a way of drawing attention to the elementary but metaphysical (there's that word again, forgive me) aspect of news reports—to the way journalism is received in the mind of the reader. Both journalist and reader bring living energies of mental association to the subject at hand and to the suggestions with which it teems, all of which among other things may argue for journalistic simplicity, for facts that are "hard" and unadorned, so that the truth of the story may be communicated strongly and simply and without being misunderstood. Ulysses Grant's orders, written in the heat and turbulence of battle, were famous for their clarity.

All depends upon the intention of the journalism, the report, the story. If the intent is to warn people of an impending invasion, say, then hard facts are called for: How far away is the invading army, how many of them are there, how are they armed, how fast are they approaching? Hard news.

At such a moment, you don't want to hear about Joan Didion's fragile nerves or about Norman Mailer's obsessions (which were often unpleasant anyway). You want hard facts.

No one understood all of this better, or earlier, than Herodotus of Halicarnassus (c. 484–c. 425 BC)—Father of History and Father of Journalism, too; and also, as many said, the Father of Lies. He believed you must not only record those facts that you absolutely know to be true (the doctrine of his near-contemporary Thucydides) but must also tell what people believe to have happened. The writer (historian-journalist) must understand people's customs, mindsets, religions, fears, hopes, ways of marrying or burying their dead, ways of making war or caring for the sick; must try to grasp, in short, the environment of their thoughts and habits and culture—their dreams, the way that their minds naturally work as they go about their lives. ■

CHAPTER 15

I miss the typewriters, although I do not use one anymore.

One day in the 1980s, I walked along West 51st Street with Otto Friedrich, heading for lunch at one of those French restaurants in Hell's Kitchen that now have mostly been replaced by skyscrapers.

I was telling Otto, excitedly, about what had happened that morning. Walter Isaacson, who was then the deputy Nation editor of the magazine, had shown me how to use the new Atex computer system that was being installed at *Time*. Walter was an enthusiast, and in his soft New Orleans accent he ran me through the wonders of the new machine—showing me the commands with which to create a file on the dark green screen and then to manipulate it with the cursor—defining blocks of text, cutting, moving, pasting, deleting sentences and paragraphs in ways that made clumps of words lighter than air and quicker than thought. I was instantly converted, like Mr. Toad when he first encountered the motorcar. It was a new world. And a miraculous toy. A quantum leap.

Otto listened to all this with a disgusted expression on his face. I noticed it and asked, "What's wrong? Do you object to the computers?"

He eyed me sourly and said, "They're not real!"

Otto refused to use the new computers at *Time*. The editor gave him a special dispensation to go on writing on his banged-up Royal manual desk model.

Otto and I had been raised in the world of typewriters and we belonged to it. It was our natural world—stipulating of course that that meant manual typewriters, never the electric. I despised electric typewriters. They emitted an insistent, irritating hum and had a jerky, alien, neurotic life of their own and a hair trigger—a key would detonate at the slightest touch, would fire off if you merely breathed on it or accidentally gave it a twitch. No good for writers, I thought, who tended to be physical with their machines and liked to twiddle the keys nervously and knead the machine's shoulders when in the anguish of composition; if they were ready for the machine actually to write something, they would tell it to do so by hitting the desired sequence of keys. We did not expect the machine to start writing on its own. The writer's brain was enough; he did not want the machine to have a brain as well—or a set of nerves that had it behaving like Blanche DuBois. The electric was liable to fire off unbidden and then you'd impatiently x out the error—or else resort to messy Wite-Out (the "liquid correction fluid" that demanded an operation as prissy as painting one's toenails). I never knew a writer who used Wite-Out except in dire necessity, such as when composing an application for a bank loan. If it was an important document, he'd yank the paper out of the machine and crumple it and toss it and start again by cranking in a fresh sheet. The floor around a writer's chair and desk was littered with crumpled pages.

I knew a writer, Greg Jaynes, who, if he made even one mistake in typing, would retype the entire page. Late at night, Greg paced the halls of the twenty-fourth floor of the Time-Life Building, muttering to himself, composing the story in his head. When he had the whole thing fixed in his mind, he would sit down and type it out—except that, as I said, he would retype any page that had a typo on it, even if he made the mistake in the last word of the last sentence. (Greg abruptly quit his job at *Time* late one night when he saw that an editor had inserted an instruction in the margin of his story: "Say something funny here.")

Another friend, Ted Morgan, wrote voluminous biographies (Franklin Delano Roosevelt, William Burroughs, and others) on a Canon Typestar—the lightweight, battery-operated electronic machine that was always my favorite, halfway between a typewriter and a word processor: deft and fast, with a sweet, lightning touch. If Ted made a typo, he retyped the entire page. There was method in this. With each retyping, he rethought the page; perfectionism in typing helped to perfect the writing.

I thought the Canon Typestar represented the best of both worlds, the old and the new. I used to know the poet James Dickey, and when

I visited him at his house in Columbia, South Carolina, I found that he kept several Typestars deployed here and there, so that if a thought occurred to him while he passed between, say, bedroom and kitchen, he might pause and tap it out on the nearest machine.

The Typestar had a small rectangular window that displayed a running digital readout of four or five words of the sentence you were composing; but it gave you paper text in the old-fashioned way: As you reached the end of each line on the electronic display, the machine printed it out on your paper, using a ribbon cartridge.

Mostly, I used a manual, desk model or portable. The keys made a *slapslapslap . . . slapslap* sound against the paper on the machine's hard rubber platen, and at the end of every line, there came a vaguely sacramental *ching!* At that signal, the left hand swept the carriage back to the right with a jaunty throw so that another line might instantly commence. This went on for years and years: I clattered out millions of words—hard rain on a tin roof. Not quite loud enough to be hail.

As a young man, my father had covered the White House and Congress for the *Philadelphia Inquirer*, whose Washington bureau was housed in the National Press Building, on 14th Street NW. One of his drinking buddies was Sammy Thompson, the telegrapher who typed the bureau's stories on a keyboard that sent the copy over the wire to the home office in Philadelphia. Sammy was short and round, a beach ball of a man, and his fat, stubby fingers were lightning fast. His thousands of keystrokes blurred together, hands like the wings of a hummingbird.

I watched Sammy at work at the bureau one Saturday morning when I was six years old, tagging along with my father when he went to the office to file a column for the Sunday paper. Sammy's fingers fascinated me—the blur of the fingers and the syncopated bounce of his fat rump upon his chair, which rolled a little upon its tiny wheels, this way and that, as the paragraphs tumbled on and his shoulders and elbows danced.

Years later, when I taught myself to type by copying articles out of the *Washington Post* without looking at the keys, I became interested in the illogic of the QWERTY layout and (more mysterious still) the way that one's typing fingers would go on automatic pilot and would find the right keys in rapid succession to make words and sentences without conscious thought: The brain's electricity fired through the fingers and the fingers brought the machine to life.

Sammy's keyboard produced a flow of rich, low tapping—a sound that might be rendered as *cluckcluckcluckcluckcluck*. A typewriter produced a noise in a slightly higher, metallic register: The typewriter (always a manual, never an electric, for the electric machine was an instrument for the business office and, as such, was merely ordinary, without mystique) would make that satisfying slap of metal upon paper that confirmed the transfer of a word from the mind to the written page. In full performance (sentences, paragraphs), this was *slapslapslap ... slap ... slapslap ... slapslap ... ching!* It was the noise of typewriters that to me was the sound of someone engaged in the hard and actually physical work of thinking. When I was a child, I might wake in the middle of the night to the sound of a typewriter faintly clacking in another part of the house.

I was a physical sort of typist. I struck the keys with a commotion of arms and elbows, like an athlete or like a concert pianist, with body English and a dancing of eyebrows, a sequence of grimaces—making faces like an actor in a silent movie: a mostly unconscious performance that captured the art and labor of the writing. If the writing was going well, I would clap my hands together loudly from time to time—a release of tension that later would remind me of how Shintoist Japanese would awaken the spirits in the landscape by clapping their hands.

Trained typists typed more calmly than I, elbows held against the rib cage, the words emerging from the subdued and disciplined action of all eight fingers (ASDF for the left hand, JKL: for the right), thumbs flick-tapping the spacebar and wrists flexing up and down in prim, monotonous rhythm, like pumpjacks on a blank page of landscape in the oil fields of West Texas. This was a deadpan style of typing that conserved physical energy but suggested the steno pool and proclaimed that the words being typed came from the mind of someone other than the typist. Novelists and poets and old-fashioned newspapermen typed with more flamboyance, sometimes with two forefingers, hunting and pecking, in a rapid fury when the muse got excited. I use the four fingers of the left hand but, for some reason, only three fingers of the right. I hit the keys hard. My shoulders get involved. Or they did once upon a time. I have not touched a typewriter in years.

∾

An aside about hearing the sounds of words as you write them down:

The word that I used a moment ago is pronounced gri-MACES, not GRIM-aces—the pronunciation is important if, like me, you hear the words in your mind as you write: if you feel their cadence. My phrase "sequence of grimaces" works only if the reader hears the accent on the MACES and pronounces the word with a long A, not a short one: gri-MACE. Attention to such a point belongs, I know, to an archaic fussiness that was instinctive long ago to certain writers but now, out of its time, seems preposterous. These are the secrets of music that, as Kenkō would have said, no one cares about anymore.

∾

The words (black ink, the typewriter typeface, disorderly, jumpy on the uppercase letters, with words x-ed out, with typos, with the raw authenticity of the old way) will last as long as the yellowing paper holds out. Copy paper of the old newspaper grade—cheap and crumbly, the kind we used at the *Evening Star* when I was a kid—will turn to dust a generation or two after the newspaperman's flesh has disintegrated. Journalism is rarely immortal.

One reason to write—or anyway, the reason that I am writing now—is to remember things. My old dog's face has turned white. Teddy is a brilliant police reporter of the woods; he knows what each animal had for dinner, for breakfast. He knows what all the creatures were up to in the middle of the night. He's a good detective. If there's a deer corpse, he knows how it happened. He can follow the trail of the killer.

I am enveloped here on my upstate farm in an environment of coyotes and deer and bobcats and bears and field mice and, in the farmhouse, of quietly decaying paper. Books by the hundreds fill walls of shelves, and my old notebooks and manuscripts piled among them, in no particular order but randomly, so that notes from 1973 (too much smoking and too much everything, all that hectic headlong life; Vietnam heading for its disreputable finish; now Watergate, Nixon in trouble, and notes on the time I sat up all night to read the galleys of *All the President's Men* with Carl Bernstein and Nora Ephron at their kitchen table in the apartment in Washington's Adams Morgan neighborhood when they had just moved in together, before they were married, and I came to visit and slept a few nights on their couch) are jumbled together with, for example, notebook after notebook of interviews from Jerusalem and Gaza and Nablus and Ramallah. And if I merely look at the place and date on the spiral notebook's front-cover label, I see, again, the urgent Palestinian men, the single Marlboro cigarette held delicately between thumb and forefinger as it is offered to the American stranger-journalist in the cool Arab house, the thimbles of sweet Turkish coffee, and the big dominant photograph high on the white, cool wall of the Dome of the Rock, golden against a sky of purest blue: fervors and bitter memories of what they call the Nakba, the disaster, in 1948, when the Jews came and, as the Arabs say, evicted them. Jamil Hamad, *Time*'s Palestinian stringer, translates and I write down the men's life stories and grievances in a rapid looping scrawl, in a sort of shorthand, not exact but seeded with clues that are meant to jog and elaborate my recollections later on, when I sit down at the typewriter.

The Israeli and Palestinian memories that I gathered in those months became for me a paradigm of all the problems of the journalistic narrative lines—the deep choices that you find at the core of stories. How do you judge them? Which are true? Are both of them—all of them—true?

Their memories become my memories for a moment—memories proliferating, Fibonacci expansions, compilations. Philosophers who think about time—what it is, how it works—refer to the growing block theory: The past is conceived as an ever-expanding block of experience and memory breeding out of the burgeoning past to form the complex, formidable present as it advances, bravely and obliviously, toward the black, blank, as-yet-uncreated future.

Nearby among my notebooks, I find the counternarrative, a hundred interviews with Israeli Jews—old people from the Holocaust and children born after the war, of parents from Treblinka who met at the displaced persons camp; the IDF colonel whose parents, though he was their "miracle child," gave him up, to be raised by other Jews on a kibbutz because their own spirits had been so blackened and murdered by the Nazis and they were terrified of infecting the child with their deadness, their darkness; or the sweet youth from the kibbutz up by the Golan Heights; or the madman I met in Hebron, the one with the closet filled with automatic weapons. So many years later, I remember him with a little chill—his eyes that were dead yet gleamed with light from another world (that of death). He had made his way to Israel from Mexico. He said he wanted to kill every Arab in the world.

The notebook pages are cluttered with approximations, crude signals from other times. My scrawled notes stir adjacent memories—they fire sleeping neurons, surprises of recall. Just now, out of nowhere (like an unexpected migrating bird come to settle for a moment in the garden), my mind is filled with a minutely detailed scene on a street corner in Khan Yunis, in Gaza. It is 1988. I stand talking with Jamil Hamad (the stringer, my friend, my drinking companion, although as a Muslim he is forbidden to touch alcohol and his wife Raida frets when he drinks and hounds him to return to the pieties), on the corner outside a small grocery store with a battered metal sign in Arabic. Wet, cold winter day. January. Palestinian men in clusters watch us at a hostile distance. It is early in the days of the first intifada. When we are driving the roads, the shebab throw stones at us. But Jamil smiles, as if to say boys will be boys, and waves to them as if he were their jolly uncle come for a visit. We have a big "PRESS" sign on the front windshield and a conspicuous galabiya draped on the dash and blue (Palestinian) license plates. So the boys abate their fury and throw the stones in an amiable, satirical way, not quite intending to hurt or damage, but rather as a gesture, a sort of theater.

On the corner by the threadbare grocery, the Arab men watch and I, like a fool, light a cigar. I liked cigars in those days, and so, in miserable Gaza, I light a big cigar. My smelly cigar fumes hang in the wet gray air and the Arab men look at me with hatred, with glowing eyes.

One of them speaks to me in a voice very low, full of intimate menace, as if to say that pretty soon he means to murder me: "Hey, Cigar Man…"

When we leave Gaza, passing an Israeli checkpoint, Jamil mutters, "Heil, Hitler!"

"*Heu, heu*!" said the ancient Romans. Which means "Alas!" ∎

CHAPTER 16

The Russians have two words for truth. Rather, they have two different words for two different kinds of truth. *Pravda* is man's truth; *istina* is God's truth. Something like that.

Pravda refers to hard, quotidian, worldly facts. Pravda tends to be a cynic. Pravda tells you that bacon sells for $3.42 a pound at Walmart; or that a Spanish Marxist named Ramón Mercader sank an ice ax in the skull of Leon Trotsky in Coyoacán, a suburb of Mexico City, on August 20, 1940, and that Trotsky (né Lev Bronstein, as *Time* magazine said now and then when its foreign editor, Laird Goldsborough, was feeling anti-Semitic in the 1930s) died of his wound in the hospital two days later. Just the facts. Istina refers to the essential truth of things, the inner truth, the poetic truth. Istina would like to know whether Trotsky was a saint or a monster and is curious to know how it happened that Saul Bellow showed up at the hospital as the great man lay dying—a somewhat bizarre and unexpected encounter that Bellow described in *The Adventures of Augie March*. (The fatuous Laird Goldsborough, by the way, was removed from his important post as *Time*'s foreign editor by Henry Luce as the 1930s grew darker; Goldsborough never recovered from the demotion, and at last, a decade later, in the midst of the Cold War, he leaped to his death from a window in the old Time-Life Building. All the way down to the pavement, he clutched his gold-headed cane.)

Trotsky—a sometime journalist all his life, by the way, and a superb writer whose memoirs read like a nineteenth-century Russian novel—used to observe that such and such an event was "unforeseen but not accidental." The mystic workings of history! Istina is something of a mystic, is capable of wonder and dread. Istina might also have a sense of humor; it might entertain you with the fact that the killer, Ramón Mercader, pretended to be a writer and that, in order to gain access to Trotsky on that day, asked him if he would look over a political screed that he had written; Trotsky consented, and as the great man sat at his desk editing the piece, Mercader did what every writer has always wished to do to his editor at one time or other: He sank an ice ax in his skull.

You might sort out journalists as either pravda people or istina people.

The police reporter is a pravda man. My dog Ted's nose works on the pravda principle. One might say that I, by contrast, belong to the istina school—as much out of laziness, I suppose, as out of mystical inclination. (Pravda is hard work: It demands details and double-checking.)

Joan Didion seemed an istina type, even though she wrote in one of her pieces that she was incapable of abstract thought. (Interesting that Joan Didion and Carl Bernstein were friends and that both of them claimed, when writing of their school studies long ago, that they could not make head or tail of Milton's *Paradise Lost*, which is the ultimate in majestic literary abstraction.)

Didion, I think, had happened onto a secret: The istina truth is not necessarily abstract. It may be that she was the perfect practitioner of pravda-as-istina, in that she got at an essence of things by understanding, by registering, as she did, the surfaces of places or persons or events, the strangeness of the concrete details: Joan Didion's surfaces had a way of leading one down into depths. Or, anyway, of inducing eerie, unexpected perceptions. She did what a good writer or journalist may do—she made you see the world in new ways. Her oddities of juxtaposition, the terror in certain concrete banalities and surprises, disclosed uncanny, forbidding California: the rattlesnake in the mailbox, the king snake on the seat of the yellow Corvette at Malibu. In Didion, there is always, somewhere in the background, the story of the Donner party (that dire American origin myth). Didion's ancestors traveled from Missouri with the original Donner party in the fall of 1846, but they split off on a different trail before the Donners went up to their fatal pass in the Sierra Nevada.

The pravda of the Donner story is known. But what is the istina of it? What is the meaning of it? That's what istina tries to get at: the inner meaning. The Rosebud. What was it Nikita Khrushchev said about the outcome of the Cuban Missile Crisis—all life wants to live? The cannibals on Robinson Crusoe's island were ceremonial in their revels; unlike the Donner party, they did not need to eat human flesh in order to survive. Cannibalism was, in their case, a sort of religious practice—or at any rate, a rite of their culture, a holiday like Thanksgiving. Poor Crusoe, at first outraged by the savagery, decided upon reflection that he had no right to judge the cannibals; they were following their customs, or, as James Fenimore Cooper's Hawkeye said of the Iroquois ways (which included torture and such), their "gifts."

One could write a book about that—Cooper's use of the word "gifts." Gifts from whom? From God? Was cannibalism a gift from God?

Henry Luce sought in his magazines to combine pravda and istina. He wrote to his parents, when he was still in his teens, that he wanted to become a journalist because "by that way I can come closest to the heart of the world." That was an istina thought. And yet he was obsessive about facts. His first title for *Time* magazine was *Fact*. And his enemies said *Time* always got the facts wrong.

I refer you again to Herodotus. He was a globe-trotting reporter. He would travel to the ends of the known world to verify a fact. It was his method to write of a given people's "gifts": their customs, their peculiarities, even their ways of urinating (among the Egyptians, he noted, women urinated standing up and men, squatting—a natural enough procedure if one considered the long robe that both sexes wore, the galabiya). Herodotus, like many great journalists, had a genius for digression. He allowed himself to pause, sometimes for pages at a time, to pick flowers by the roadside.

Journalistic oddments are everywhere in Herodotus:

"The Babylonians have no doctors, but bring their invalids out into the street, where anyone who comes along offers the sufferer advice on his complaint, either from personal experience or observation of a similar complaint in others."

And this: "The Atarantes [people in the interior of Africa] are the only people in the world . . . to do without names. Atarantes is the collective name—but individually they have none. They curse the sun as it arises and call it by all sorts of opprobrious names, because it wastes and burns both themselves and their land."

And the Lydians: "[Their] way of life, aside from the fact that they prostitute their daughters, is not unlike our own."

Twenty-five hundred years after Herodotus, Gay Talese collected such oddments in his pieces, such as one entitled "New York Is a City of Things Unnoticed" that he wrote for the *New York Times*:

> Most popcorn chewers at Yankee Stadium stop chewing momentarily just before the pitch. Gum chewers on Macy's escalators stop chewing momentarily just before they get off—to concentrate on the last step... On Broadway in the evening, a big, dark 1948 Rolls-Royce pulls in—and out hops a little lady armed with a Bible and a sign reading "The Damned Shall Perish." She proceeds to stand on the corner screaming at the multitudes of Broadway sinners sometimes until 3 A.M., when the chauffeur-driven Rolls picks her up and drives her back to Westchester... The mannequins [in the display windows] at Peck & Peck are made to look young and prim, while at Lord & Taylor they seem wiser and windblown. At Saks they are demure but mature, while at Bergdorf's they look agelessly elegant and quietly rich. The profiles of Fifth Avenue's mannequins have been fashioned after some of the world's most alluring women— women like Suzy Parker, who posed for the Best & Co. mannequins, and Brigitte Bardot, who inspired some mannequins at Saks.

Talese's portrait of Frank Sinatra, published in Esquire ("Frank Sinatra Has a Cold") is as good as any biography in Plutarch's *Parallel Lives*—and employs some of the same techniques, especially in the accumulation of anecdotes, minutely detailed. ∎

CHAPTER 17

Harry Luce was a preeminent American mythmaker of the twentieth century. Is a mythmaker to be trusted as a journalist? Or are those two roles (the making of myths and the accurate reporting of facts) entirely irreconcilable?

It is a question that goes to the nature of storytelling and narrative lines and even to what might be called the culture of the storyteller's psyche: its biases. Think about the difference between John Hersey and Walter Duranty—who were thought to be, respectively, the best and the worst journalist of the twentieth century and who were both, in opposite directions, mythmakers. The tale of each of those men turns upon the question of the narrative line, the story that each fashioned out of the tremendous historical facts that he confronted—the terrible Ukrainian famine and Hiroshima.

Luce, too, should be understood in terms of the moral and political storylines that were distinctive and controversial in his magazines. He was, I suspect, the most important journalist of the twentieth century. I'm not sure who was the greatest.

Luce was the old America, the twentieth-century version—the America before the very different America that we have now. He expressed—and his magazines manifested—the dominant, middle-class American civilization from, let us say, the stock market crash in 1929 to the fall of Saigon in 1975. When voices in the twenty-first century chant "Hey hey, ho ho, Western Civ has got to go," they mean to repudiate an evolution of the American mind that was, in its essence, indistinguishable from the mind of Henry Luce—a well-educated, civilized white male of wealth and power whose magazines were the gold standard in the golden age of magazines. Through them, Luce undertook to tell Americans who

they were and what they thought. The magazines—especially *Time*—
practiced a vivid, opinionated brand of journalism that Luce's numerous
foes called propaganda, or worse.

His enemies were fierce, none more so than his biographer W.A.
Swanberg, whose 1972 portrait in a book called *Luce and His Empire*—
published five years after Luce's death—was a hatchet job in which
(with fitting symmetry) Swanberg committed every sin of which he
accused Luce: gross distortion, sneering innuendo, outright falsehood.
Intellectuals hated Luce, in part because they envied him his enormous
readership and influence over the American public, and in part because
of the embarrassed memory of their own political mistakes in the 1930s
and later—for example, their infatuations with Stalin or Trotsky and with
the promise of the Soviet paradise and salvation-by-Communism. Luce
was right about those matters, and they could not forgive him for that.

Luce was wrong sometimes—about Vietnam, about other things. But
his greatness as a journalist had nothing to do with politics or ideology.
His enemies never properly made that distinction between his politics
and his gifts as a journalist. He was a moderate Republican whom they
described, inaccurately, as a "reactionary." (He aggressively supported—
all but sponsored—the presidential candidacy of Wendell Willkie in
1940 and of Dwight Eisenhower in 1952. Neither of those men was even
remotely reactionary; they weren't even politicians.)

Luce's skills as a journalist were formidable. He was probably a better reporter than anyone who worked for him—and his correspondents
and editors were among the best (some of them). His magazines *Time*,
Fortune, and *Life* were brilliant inventions—advances of the magazine
form in three separate directions during the great age of magazines. He
vastly enlarged the very idea of news and the scope and ambitions of
journalism. Time Life became an iconic American brand, like U.S. Steel.

People who grew up in the age of the internet have little conception
of the role that magazines once played in American culture and politics—
even, one might say, in the American psyche. And the magazines of Henry
Luce (especially *Time*, *Life*, and *Fortune*) were the ones that, because of
their extraordinarily high quality and wide circulation, made the deepest
impression upon the American middle class. (His enemies, reading my

line about the Luce magazines' "extraordinarily high quality," would have indignantly denied it; smoke would have come out of their ears.)

☙

Luce didn't exactly laugh; he chuckled, and the chuckle had a little edge of knowingness and rue. He was not a mirthful or an angry or a luxurious or a venal man. If you had asked him if he was happy, he would have been surprised and would have asked, "What's that got to do with it?"

He is forgotten now. He died in Phoenix in 1967, of a heart attack in a house beside a golf course, at the height of the Vietnam War. It was said that he exclaimed, "Oh, God!" and fell to the bathroom floor. It wasn't clear whether that "Oh, God!" was a prayer or a profanity. ∎

CHAPTER 18

I never met Luce. Everyone called him Harry, everyone except Franklin Roosevelt, who feared his power and disliked him and called him Henry just to irritate him. Luce retired a year before I arrived at *Time* in 1965. All through the sixties and seventies, I disliked him; I mean that I disliked the idea of the man, even as I worked for the magazine that was his invention and his darling.

Gradually, I came to think better of him. He had a way of being vindicated by the passage of years. But after his death, his magazine empire, once the mightiest in the world, fell eventually into the hands of lesser mortals and, down the decades, passed through evolutions and misadventures. It was never the same, either morally or editorially, after he was gone, and anyway the world and the country were much changed—until at last, in 2018, it was broken up.

After that happened, I wrote this elegy:

Henry Luce's America died about the same time that Luce did. In later times, it would reappear only to be satirized as a remnant of the age of *Mad Men*—the regime of white, male, privileged characters who drank like fish and smoked like chimneys and treated women as if, officially speaking, they did not quite exist.

At the time, it did not occur to Luce and his men to think of themselves as white or male or privileged; the politics of identity lay in the future. Luce was a journalistic genius, and his sense of the world was portentous, preoccupied by world wars and the rise and fall of empires. He invented "the American Century," and people derided him for the phrase. They said that, like the man himself, it was overbearing, arrogant. He was a little surprised at that. He never quite understood why people hated him. He knew that he had meant well. He did not mean "the American Century" in a proprietary way (which is how it was taken) but rather as a statement of what he took to be his mighty nation's moral responsibility in a world torn apart by world war and fascism and communism—the active, ruthless energies of un-freedom and un-democracy.

His many enemies on the left—including a number of his own editors and writers—considered him a reactionary and a horse's ass who was either sinister or endearing, depending on their mood at the time that they were telling stories about him. One of his top editors said, "He was not a likable man, but there was something lovable about him, if you know what I mean." Anyway, he seemed too powerful.

Luce tended to be underestimated and misinterpreted and to be unfairly blamed for all sorts of things because he was rich and successful and Republican and given to making large pronouncements. He worshipped heroes; he dined on Big Ideas. He chain-smoked cigarettes: smoke exploded from his mouth in blue-gray bursts. He was always running out of cigarettes and bumming them from his editorial courtiers (his "housecarls," as John Kenneth Galbraith called them). After he had taken a cigarette from someone else's pack, he might abstractedly pocket the pack, all the while talking, talking. Sometimes, when he talked, it sounded as if he were barking…

He also kept the matches.

In the midst of conversation—at lunch en famille with his editors, for example (those communal meals being a sort of sacrament at Time Inc.)—he would fall abruptly into formidable silence, and the editors would wait, like whale-watchers when the whale has sounded. It was against the rules for the others to speak while Harry Luce was thinking. He vanished into the deep…Minutes might pass in that still suspension…

And then the whale would breach: Luce would erupt and resume his spouting, bounding monologue, chasing ideas over the open sea.

☙

John Bunyan's Pilgrim—Christian—was often rude to people in the way that Luce was rude. Bunyan's Christian was rude because he carried a Burden of Sin and because he was intent upon overcoming all obstacles and temptations in order to reach the Heavenly City. Christian was especially rude when he found himself in places like Vanity Fair, with its gaudy distractions and temptations.

Luce made his headquarters in the twentieth century's Vanity Fair, in bristling, venal Manhattan, a few miles north of Wall Street, in Rockefeller Center, or else a couple blocks to the east, on Park Avenue, at the Waldorf Astoria, where he kept a penthouse apartment for a time and in whose ballrooms his magazines often held their fancy ceremonial banquets.

Woodrow Wilson praised "the South and West with their simpler life, their scattered people, their fields of grain, their mines of metal, their little towns...No country ought ever to be judged from its seething centers."

Luce ran his magazines from New York, the "seething center" of American business and media. He belonged to the city and to its best clubs, and yet he was somewhat curiously always an outsider there: It was, after all, Vanity Fair, and something in his Presbyterian self was bound to abhor it, and he agreed with Wilson that the authentic America lay west of the Hudson. New York was a distortion, a temptation, a mirage.

He prodded his writers and editors to get out into the country and to understand that the New York and Washington points of view were not reliable, that real America was not in Washington or New York but was to be found out there, out in the country. At editorial lunches at the top of the Time-Life Building, it was a familiar ploy for an editor to support an argument by mentioning that he had just returned from Kansas City or Duluth, and out there—that is, out among the real people, the real Americans—the sentiment was such and such. A Howard Hawks comedy in 1941, *Ball of Fire*, starring Barbara Stanwyck and Gary Cooper, satirized the idea of isolated eggheads—lexicographers—talking wistfully about the real world. Luce's writers and editors in the Time-Life Building sometimes felt that way, yammering and full of theories, cooped up in a fancy headquarters building and cut off from the "real world." Once in a somewhat mawkish speech to his senior people, Luce had confessed that he wished that when someone asked him his hometown, he could reply,

"Oskaloosa, Iowa" (instead of Tengchow, China). In some ways of course, this idealizing of Oskaloosa was silly—romantic nonsense like that of the nineteenth-century Russian intelligentsia (Narodniki) who romanticized the primitive life of the "real Russia," which was often enough a story of drunken ignorance, wife-beating brutality, and poverty.

This was one of the great Luce binaries—New York vs. the Real America—a variation on the binary upon which politicians play every four years: unreal Washington (corrupt etc.) vs. Real America.

Another cranky genius of the American magazine, Harold Ross, started the *New Yorker* in 1925, two years after Briton Hadden and Luce founded *Time*. Ross was an endearing rube, or pseudo-rube, who was raised in small-town Colorado and Utah. He said, "The *New Yorker* will be the magazine which is not edited for the old lady in Dubuque."

Here was another binary system: Ross's Dubuque vs. Luce's Oskaloosa.

ɞ

It was at an Elsa Maxwell ball for Cole Porter at the Waldorf Astoria in 1934 that Luce left his faithful wife of eleven years, Lila, and ran off with the beautiful managing editor of *Vanity Fair*—that is, Condé Nast's *Vanity Fair*, not John Bunyan's. That night, at least, was the beginning of the affair. She was entirely a creature of New York and its glamour. Luce's friends and colleagues—including the poet Archibald MacLeish, who was *Fortune*'s star writer—were astonished. Luce called it a "coup de foudre"—a smiting and transformative case of puppy love that, to Luce, because he was Luce, seemed as significant as the illumination that struck the apostle Paul on the road to Damascus. The woman's name was Clare Boothe Brokaw. Harry and Clare married and became a famous couple. Their glamorous public marriage would, in time, become a private disaster—bitter, melancholy. And yet, to the end, there remained between them a tenderness, a respect, a sort of thwarted awe. Clare Luce was hard on Harry. He maddened her and she drove him crazy. She told a story about how she bought a beautiful new gown to wear at some memorable ball. She modeled it for Harry one evening when he got home from the

Time-Life Building and asked, "How do you like it?" He flicked a distracted glance in her direction and said, "Yes, lovely, dear. That's always been one of my favorites." When she told the story, Clare said, "What do you do with a man like that?" She said he wasn't very good in bed. Clare was like that.

She took lovers. So did he. Late in life he fell in love with Lord Beaverbrook's niece, Lady Jeanne Campbell, a woman much younger than he, and they had a wistful, May-December love affair (she wrote a sad poem to him whose refrain was, "I am young, and you are old"). They would spend a few hours in the afternoon in her little apartment on the Upper East Side, and you thought of Cordelia and Lear, birds in a cage. But by then—this was in the latter part of the 1950s—Luce was not well (heart trouble). He feared a public scandal (the old goat and the ingenue—not so different, perhaps, from the "love-nest" scandal that overtook Charles Foster Kane in the movie) would irreparably damage his beloved Time Inc. Clare, who had become a Catholic some years earlier, knew of the affair and threatened suicide if he left her. It was a horrible mess. Harry gave up Jeanne and returned to Clare. Jeanne, on the rebound, married Norman Mailer—a very foolish thing to do. That marriage lasted less than a year.

For all of their troubles, Harry was proud of Clare—of her intellect and work—and when President Eisenhower sent her to Rome as American ambassador, he uprooted his corporate life and went along to Italy as her dutiful consort and helper.

Justice Oliver Wendell Holmes was reported to have said that Franklin Roosevelt had "a second-class intellect but a first-class temperament." Luce was the reverse. He had a first-class intellect but a second-class temperament.

Luce was a lean, off-handsome man with thinning hair and gray-blue eyes—narrowed wolf's eyes that emitted a glacial light. His eyebrows were dense and seemed to grow wild. They looked like shrubbery, or like thunderclouds. His nose turned up slightly at the tip. He had a warlord's air. His impressive head suggested alertness, wariness, fortification, discipline. He bristled with energy, an electric aura—a radiation of power that had in it, as power does, an organizing core of narcissism. A sardonic intelligence.

Luce stuttered badly when he was young and as a grown man gave an impression of suppression and enjambment. His handwriting was clear, strong, and regular, leaning urgently to starboard.

His inclinations were grandiose and high-handed and autocratic, and yet, at the same time, he judged himself harshly. He may have been doubly rude to his underlings because he sensed that he himself had become morally second-rate (his magazines had their vulgarities, and they pandered to the sinners, and he took good money for all those liquor and cigarette ads) and because he had failed to live up to his parents' standard of virtue and had chosen to make a comfortable life in the Vanity Fair of American money instead of laboring in some hard missionary school in China, where a part of him considered that he ought to be. Instead of itinerating among peasants by the swollen Yangtze River, where millions might die because of a flood or a bad harvest year, there he was having lunch with the rich and powerful at the Union League Club.

But sometimes he struck people as shy, unsure of himself. William F. Buckley Jr. had that impression one night when they sat together at a formal dinner in New York. "Luce seemed almost blank," Buckley told me. "Diffident. He puzzled me. He had a way of disappearing. This seemed strange. I found him a difficult man to focus upon. He kept going out of range. Some thought he might be weak. They said his mouth seemed weak." Some thought he looked like Frank Morgan playing the Wizard of Oz. There was a story that one night he and Clare organized a cocktail party in New York, inviting a lot of fancy and powerful guests; and before the people started showing up, it was said he fretted and worried and said, "What if they don't come?"

But as a fact-gathering journalist, he proceeded with the ferocious, candid naivete that makes a great reporter. He was never afraid to ask a question—was never embarrassed or worried that the question would make him look stupid. John Hersey said, "His most attractive trait was his delight in finding out something he had not known before." He was, in that sense—despite what his enemies said and despite all the uproar of politics that surrounded his career—a model of the world-class journalist. His eyes were searching and penetrating and shrewd, and his reading of other people was subtle and sure and confident. He was simultaneously inner-directed and outer-directed—another of his binaries.

Imps of contradiction scurried about.

If you saw him off duty, he could be the nicest guy—a sweet man with a capacity for tenderness, with instinctive courtesy. He was both shy and ruthless. He struck people as single-minded; yet he presided over a multiple self. He could be self-effacing, endearing. His daughters-in-law were half in love with him. One of his favorite *Time-Life* writers—until the Hiss case came along in 1948—was the doomy, melodramatic apostate Communist Whittaker Chambers, whose anguished sainthood appealed to Luce's memory of a religious childhood. Even more than Luce, Chambers saw the news, the immense, unfolding story of the world, in a literary and religious light. Journalism, to Chambers, became (as the title of his great memoir, *Witness*, suggested) an urgently spiritual business: the salvation or damnation of the world might depend upon it.

 e⁄ɔ

I suspect Luce's bad manners may have been in part a managerial technique. A man running a big company may find that brusque, high-handed clarity—rudeness, if you like—is sometimes more effective than the time-consuming courtesies. Joseph Conrad wrote in one of his novellas "I have known the sea too long to believe in its respect for decency. An elemental force is ruthlessly frank." Luce's hostile biographer Swanberg would write him off as, on the one hand, a sinister, elemental force in American life and culture and, on the other hand, a petty tyrant (abuser of waiters and other little people) and a hopeless bore. Swanberg, a Socialist out of 1930s Minnesota, hated Luce—considered him the Prospero of capitalist disinformation and hypocrisy.

Swanberg's idea of the great American hero (and the subject of his last biography) was Norman Thomas, the white-haired and aristocratic grand old man of American Socialism, who ran for president on the Socialist ticket every election year from 1928 to 1948, in a repetitive ritual that came to seem like time-lapse photography. Toward the end of his long career, he was in his eighties and stooped with age; one of his routines was to appear on a stage and to shuffle, very slowly, toward the podium (a long, suspenseful journey that the audience watched in anxious silence). When Thomas finally arrived at the microphone, he would flash a grin and cry, "Creeping Socialism!" It brought down the house.

☙

I dwell on the subject of Henry Luce not only because he turned into my Charlie Kane but also, naturally, because I worked for so long at his magazine (over which, for years, his ghost presided, though gradually his influence receded and new people came on the staff and the editors whom he'd trained in the old Luce ways retired or died); and because I went back and forth in my thinking about him—admiring him sometimes, and then not. I had a hard time making up my mind; I still do. Mostly, the storyline on Henry Luce—among people at his magazines as well as elsewhere among journalists—was either hostile or dismissive. He was no one's hero. Vietnam did that—or, in a larger sense, the entire sea change of the 1960s: that immense generational changing of the guard. In an odd, contrarian way, however, he gradually became a sort of hero of mine, or something of the kind. A sort of power animal. I found that I was inclined to defend him. I never liked the 1960s anyway.

After his death, after Vietnam and all that, there came to be, at Time Inc., a distinct distaste for the founder—an ideological disapproval, a sort of embarrassment, as in the Henry James novel in which the family does not discuss the inelegant source of the family wealth. You could feel it when his name was mentioned. Many years after Luce was gone, I had lunch in a midtown restaurant with Jason McManus, who was one of his successors as editor-in-chief of Time Inc. Jason had been one of my earliest senior editors at *Time*, when I wrote in the Nation section. I asked him what Luce had been like. Jason did not hesitate. He answered with one word: "Uncouth." I was surprised. (I recalled later that when someone asked Luce his judgment of Senator Joe McCarthy of Wisconsin, he had also replied, without hesitation, "Uncouth.")

Jason went on to soften the judgment. He said that, with Luce, what you saw was what you got, and that, at least, was something in his favor.

It was clear Jason never quite liked him; he thought there was something wrong with him, something repellant.

The note of distaste for Luce would be heard throughout the empire that he founded. One day Andrew Heiskell, a top man at Time Inc. and sometime publisher of *Life*, was remembering Luce for an oral history and he happened to speak of Scranton, Pennsylvania, which was the Reverend Henry Winters Luce's birthplace and home before he set off to be a missionary in China. Heiskell referred to the city as "Scranton—that dreadful place."

Another top man, Ralph Graves, who became managing editor of *Life* and later the editorial director of Time Inc., told me a story about how Luce embarrassed him and a couple of other *Time* people one day when Luce invited himself along to their lunch at Pearl's, an excellent Cantonese restaurant on 48th Street, a favorite of *Time-Life* people, some of whom invested money in the place. Graves said that, to the chagrin of his companions and the elegant owner, Pearl Wong, Luce went on and on about how happy he was to be eating "real Chinese peasant food."

Poor Luce. Of all the stories that Ralph might have told me about him, he chose to describe that maladroit performance at a Chinese restaurant by a man who had little in the way of social skills. (One notices, by the way, how often stories about Luce involved restaurants and lunches and dinners. I wondered sometimes why that should be so. He'd waited on tables to work his way through school and so perhaps he enjoyed these public displays of being waited on. Anyway, such meals allowed him to convene an audience of writers and editors and dominate them and pump them for ideas, or else encourage them or reprove them. It's not clear that he ever enjoyed the food or drink very much himself. There were stories about how he would sit down with the editors and talk nonstop, eating his lunch in the process, but then, as if startled, would look up at the waiter and demand to know why he had not yet brought the food. He had not noticed that he had already eaten. He said food was "just fuel.")

Luce's genius elevated men like McManus and Heiskell and Graves to a certain amount of wealth and comfort and to perches in mid-Manhattan from which they felt entitled to use words like "uncouth" and "dreadful." Graves and Heiskell and McManus were other-directed, to use the sociologist's terms, and Luce was inner-directed; or, better to say, he was Luce-directed. They and Luce came from different geologic ages. Luce was a beast of the prime.

John F. Kennedy once said, "I like old Luce. He reminds me of my father. Those tough old guys made it on their own." Harry Luce and Joe Kennedy had their piratical authenticity. So did their America. Tough old Luce survived John Kennedy by four years. There were giants in the earth in those days.

But Harry Luce and Joe Kennedy were quite different characters. One night just after World War II, the two men were having dinner and discussing their sons. John Kennedy was running for Congress in Massachusetts. Luce mentioned his own son Hank (Henry Luce III), just out of the navy.

Joe Kennedy said, "Why don't you buy him a seat in Congress?"

Harry Luce was shocked. "Buy him a seat? You can't do that!"

Joe Kennedy said, "Come on, Harry. Of course, you can."

❦

This was the essence of his enemies' verdict: Luce was a malevolent naïf, a faux-innocent, a Rotarian Svengali to an America that was a little too clueless and smug and "midcult" and "bourgeois," and, frankly, too stupid to resist his magazines and their smug, midcult, bourgeois messages. He was, his enemies said, obtusely and obsessively anti-Communist. He was always putting Chiang Kai-shek or Madame Chiang on the cover of *Time* magazine. His fantasy of some sort of Christianized China (which might have vindicated his father's years of hard labor as a missionary) led, his enemies said, to the disaster of the Vietnam War.

His manners were decent and collegial, but below the surface, he consciously or unconsciously compared people with whom he dealt, in business or politics or journalism, to his parents and the other virtuous missionaries he remembered from his childhood. Those paragons, in their self-sacrifice and sweet character, made the venal, secular, merely careerist figures he encountered in adult life seem shallow and a bit contemptible. He never quite got over an idealization of his early saints and the relatively straitened lives that they had lived in the mission field, serving others. It is true he had hated the threadbare quality of the mission life and that he hated, even more, being a scholarship boy at Hotchkiss and Yale among the rich sons of bankers and industrialists. Yet he considered the missionaries to be morally superior. He starred at Hotchkiss and Yale by dint of intellect and hard work. Yet at the same time he loathed waiting on tables to pay his board, and he envied his classmates their money and social ease, their clubs and their fathers' mansions in Shaker Heights or Grosse Pointe, and the enormous headlights of their fathers' chauffeur-driven limousines.

The merely secular people, he could not help feeling, were second-rate from a moral and spiritual point of view. His employees, often first-rate professionals, might suffer in his eyes by that hidden comparison. They were second-rate in part because they took the big salaries that he lavished upon them. Unlike the missionaries, unlike his parents, they could be bought—by Luce. He treated them to the best restaurants in New York and Paris and, after they had ordered the fanciest items on the menu, he would grunt and ask the headwaiter for ketchup. ("Yes," he would say, "I know what canard a l'orange is.") There were many stories along those lines. He was a moral snob and a bit of a prig. He once advised his daughter-in-law Patty Chapman, the first wife of his son Hank, to look up the last lines of Shelley's "Prometheus Unbound," which he admired.

The lines are:

To defy Power, which seems omnipotent;
To love, and bear; to hope till Hope creates
From its own wreck the thing it contemplates;
Neither to change, nor falter, nor repent;
This, like thy glory, Titan, is to be
Good, great and joyous, beautiful and free;
This is alone Life, Joy, Empire, and Victory!

Not one to be carried away, Luce cautioned his daughter-in-law: "It's on the pagan side and needs to be corrected by the Book of Common Prayer but it's pretty wonderful."

The missionary's boy felt obliged to correct Percy Bysshe Shelley.

Luce in the early sixties experimented with LSD, partly for journalistic and partly for spiritual reasons. He did not entirely enjoy the effect—he may have gotten bored. And so, while waiting for the drug to wear off, he calmly read Lionel Trilling's life of Matthew Arnold.

I admired him for that.

❧

Mad Men was filmed in the Time-Life Building in New York. The advertising executive Don Draper's office reproduced, in eerie detail, my senior editor Gus Daniels's office as it appeared when I arrived at *Time* in summer 1965. One Saturday night that summer, we made last-minute changes on the "yellows" (the final edit before a story went to the printers) and wrote captions and waited for "checkpoints" to clatter into the wire room from correspondents in the bureaus. Everything was done on paper: computers lay far in the future. Researchers, all women, hurried in and out of the room with fixes—"red changes"—on the copy. We were gathered in Gus's office and drank Johnny Walker Red or Bombay gin (the Luce operation was famous for its good liquor).

On this particular Saturday night, we watched the Watts riots on Gus's color television set. Watts was the first of the great summer riots of the 1960s. We watched mostly in silence, except for the rattle of the ice in our glasses. We'd had three or four hours' sleep the night before—the usual routine toward the end of the editorial week. The Tower Suite sent down a catered roast beef dinner, and we went off to eat at our desks. Accounts of the old days at *Time* always made much of the liquor carts and the catered dinners and the fancy expense accounts, and all of that was true. But the work was hard and the standards, on the whole, were exacting and obsessive; the editors, sometimes spectacularly neurotic (one of them ate pieces of paper when he was agitated), were also intelligent and sometimes learned; and the people one worked with were, many of them, splendid and gifted and eccentric. Time Inc. was an interesting and demanding universe.

If we had been more alert and thoughtful about the riots and the television coverage that night in 1965, we might have felt a tremor—might have had a distant intuition of the end of days. In years to come, Time Inc. would merge with Warner, and then Time Warner would merge with AOL (a disaster). The technology and the very metaphysics of journalism would change.

Every now and then Luce reappeared in the building, like the ghost of Hamlet's father. There would be a stir along the corridors. He would vanish upstairs to have lunch with the editors in a private dining room. He was a sort of hallucination. I glimpsed him only once, as the doors of an elevator closed.

But even with Luce gone, his great work, Time Inc., remained the superpower of print. When I sat down in my office on the twenty-fifth floor to bang out a story, without byline, on one of those warhorse Royal desk-model typewriters, I was a voice in the chorus. I consoled myself with the knowledge that my words (about Vietnam, about civil rights, about Mao and his Cultural Revolution, or about the Rolling Stones and Haight-Ashbury and the Great Society and the Manson murders) would go out to a readership of millions. A motorcycle courier would speed an early copy of the magazine (a "makeready") to the White House on Sunday night. Lyndon Johnson would wait up for it in his pajamas and pore over the magazine; if he read something he didn't like (my very own words, maybe—LBJ might be furious at what I had written), he would phone Hugh Sidey, *Time*'s White House correspondent, and wake him up and yell in his ear. *Goddamn it, Sidey! You bastards! What are you trying to do to the leader of the free world?*

I knew that my story would be read by every mayor and governor in America, by every senator and congressman, every justice of the Supreme Court—by the president of each corporation, by all who were in power in America, or wished to be in power; and by every lawyer, every doctor and dentist, and by their patients in the waiting room.

That was Time Inc.'s power—the influence of *Time* and *Life*, primarily, preeminent magazines in America's long golden age of magazines that ran from early in the twentieth century until, let us say, the folding of *Life* in 1972. Luce was the Henry Ford of magazines. Born in exile—at a mission in Shandong, a world away from his birthright (the first Henry Luce had arrived in America in 1636 and started a farm on Martha's Vineyard)—he would use his magazines to invent, or reinvent, America according to his own moral and, one might say, religious design.

He and his partner/rival and classmate from Yale, Briton Hadden, came out with the first issue of *Time* in March 1923, and within five or six years, both of them were millionaires. Hadden died in 1929. Just at the start of the Depression (bad timing, one would think), Luce came forth with the opulent *Fortune*, which, in its early years, was arguably the best magazine ever published. Then in 1936, Time Inc. began publication of *Life*, another brilliant invention, the best and most successful of the picture magazines. Over the years, claimed Robert Hutchins, an educator and former chancellor of the University of Chicago, Luce's magazines would have more impact on the American mind than the country's entire system of public education. That may be true.

Henry Luce studied Greek at Hotchkiss and Yale. So did Briton Hadden. They were stars and rivals and wary friends, and both of them made Skull and Bones, Yale's secret society. Just before the crash of 1929, Hadden died of a blood infection, the scratch of a cat, evidently. There were no antibiotics at the time. If the cat had waited a few years to scratch Brit Hadden, penicillin might have saved him. *Sunt lacrimae rerum.*

Hadden called himself Caliban—that was his Skull and Bones name—and most nights when he was not getting out the magazine, he would be found at a speakeasy on Third Avenue where he held court at the bar, speaking out of the corner of his mouth in a mock-tough gangster way. Brit Hadden invented *Time*'s telegraphic, wise-guy or mock-epic style, with its prep-school erudition (inverted sentences, Homeric epithets) and its razzing way of giving a hotfoot to the mighty. In those days—long before the company was rich enough to hire correspondents and set up bureaus around the world—*Time* was a rewrite sheet, Hadden and Luce and their writers condensing and jazzing up stories they had clipped from the *New York Times* and the *Herald Tribune* and other papers (much to the annoyance of those publications and their people). ∎

CHAPTER 19

Harry Luce was two years old when the Boxers came. It was the early summer of 1900. The Boxers, officially the Society of Righteous and Harmonious Fists, emerged in waves and waves, red-sashed and fevered-up with hatred of the foreign devil; they flowed like a river in flood, across the Shandong countryside, through the villages, among the burial mounds of the ancestors.

The Boxers took Horace Tracy "Pit" Pitkin (Yale '92, old friend and classmate of the Reverend Luce and, with him, an early enthusiast of the Student Volunteer Movement) at the mission in Baoding, some miles away. The Boxers cut off Pit's head. That came as a shock to the missionaries: a sudden, biblical moment, martyrdom.

Little Harry's young mother, Elizabeth Root Luce, was pregnant with her second child, who would be named Emmavail. The Luces had known enough of the danger to keep suitcases packed beside the front door of their mission in Tengchow. Before dawn, they fled through the town, down to the harbor.

The amah bounced along in the darkness, carrying little Harry. A sympathetic Chinese gunboat captain, a Christian, took the family aboard and the boat slipped out into the Yellow Sea. The captain delivered the Luces to a ship that carried them across the water to Korea, and they waited in Seoul all summer with other missionaries temporarily stranded by the Boxers' insurrection. "What days these are for China!" the Reverend Luce wrote. "Days of suspense, days of suffering and persecution, days of blood and death! But in it all the missionaries have not lost their quiet and calm, standing firm in their determination to pour out their lives for China. I have not heard a single hopeless word spoken by one of them. God's kingdom will still be set up in China."

The empress dowager fled with her eunuchs to the summer palace ("Of the thirty-six ways to escape, running away is best" was a Chinese saying). The foreigners' armies (American, Russian, French, British, Japanese) marched into Peking to relieve the embassies and claim the Forbidden City and loot the jades. Presently the Boxers flowed back into the countryside, and, for the moment, the crisis passed. ∎

CHAPTER 20

The story of the Luces' escape from the Boxers had biblical touches—Moses in the bulrushes, the flight into Egypt.

It was a good story, with an atmosphere of myth and a hint of miracle: A child was plucked from danger in order that he might grow up and do great things in the world.

&

All of this happened at the dawn of the twentieth century. At that moment, another Henry—the aging Henry Adams (a Washington journalist in his youth, by the way)—surveyed the world and feared that the new era, however bright and noisy and smug and overconfident might be its mood at the moment, brought with it unreadable and terrifying complexities.

He was the great-grandson of President John Adams and grandson of President John Quincy Adams, and he professed to be a remnant of a more intelligible and congenial age—the eighteenth century. He predicted that the twentieth century's new energies would be satanic and would carry mankind over into a universe of the meaningless, presided over by new forces, which he summarized in his metaphor of the Dynamo—soundless and terrible.

Darwin had done his work to shake the foundations of religious faith, Freud debunked the innocence of childhood, and Einstein abolished Isaac Newton's heavenly clockwork. The old empires collapsed. Electricity turned night into day, the telephone annulled distance; the automobile, the airplane, the movies—all altered the experience of reality. They changed the nature of nature—turned the world's operating systems upside down. Predominantly rural and agricultural America morphed into industrial and urban America. Electric elevators made skyscrapers possible, and cities pivoted ninety degrees, from horizontal to vertical, and the country's genes and culture and politics were altered forever as waves of immigrants swarmed in from Eastern Europe and Italy and elsewhere. Americans who had arrived in earlier years, people with old names and embedded identities, began to feel like strangers in their own country.

But Harry Luce had also arrived from elsewhere, from the other side of the world. He, too, in a way was a stranger: an immigrant with all the advantages of the old American stock but with the fresh eye of a kind of greenhorn—and also the ambition and the hope and the connections. Luce came as an "immigrant" with all possible advantages.

"Progress" had acquired a dark side. At Ypres and the Somme, long-range artillery collaborated with machine guns that fired several hundred bullets a minute. They achieved an unthinkable productivity of death—a premonition of what was to come. A generation of Europe's young men went under. Karl Marx's new religion, its missionaries more numerous and ruthless than those of the Christians, would overturn empires (in Russia and China) and start an imperium of their own.

The nineteenth century's intellectual solidities broke up and dissolved into incoherence, or into novel, infidel meanings, or anyway a new bewilderment, motifs of disintegration and disillusion reflected in the works of Picasso and James Joyce and Stravinsky and T.S. Eliot and Lytton Strachey and distilled in whatever lessons were to be drawn from terrible actual fragmentations—corpses at Ypres and, decades later, ashes of Auschwitz and Hiroshima and Nagasaki. The previous century's big ideas (*dulce et decorum est pro patria mori* and all of that Victorian nonsense that Strachey mocked) gave place to new big ideas that broke loose in the world and, from time to time, killed millions. Physics and politics both grew totalitarian and imitated one another in organizing enormities.

The Christians went on offering their traditional messages—Christ's meanings, with European American admixtures: mere simperings, the intellectuals thought, compared to muscular Marxism. The novelist E.M.

Forster called it "poor little talkative Christianity." The Marxists offered a sinuous and ruthless new faith and orthodoxy—Marx's meanings, with Leninist or Stalinist or Trotskyist or Maoist admixtures.

The twentieth century would become an immense collision of meanings, the demolition derby of ideas. A nineteenth-century Swedenborgian named Sampson Reed had written, "All the changes which are taking place in the world originate in the mind." Systems of Meaning were apt to become totalitarian. Meaninglessness produced even greater terror. Meaning and Meaninglessness conducted a saturnine dialogue. Each was the other's evil twin.

Those would be among the century's themes.

"Where is wisdom to be found?" asked the book of Job, "and where is the place of understanding?" The book of Job, if one thought about it—God acting badly, chatting with Satan as if the two of them were racetrack touts, the Almighty acquiescing in evil and all but sponsoring it—seemed a thoroughly Modernist piece of work.

Henry Adams struggled with the terror. There was a seed of gruesome irony in this. Adams was an almost pathological anti-Semite. He died in 1918 and so he did not live to see the ways in which the twentieth century would develop that theme: Hitler's own dynamo—the SS, Auschwitz, etc.—would attempt a Final Solution.

Adams was filled with such a pessimism of expiring Christian faith that, as he wrote in *The Education of Henry Adams* (speaking of himself in the third person, as usual), "in 1900 he entered a far vaster universe, where all the old roads ran about in every direction, overrunning, dividing, subdividing, stopping abruptly, vanishing slowly in sidepaths that led nowhere, and sequences that could not be proved." Or "he struck it in everyday life as though he were still Adam in the Garden of Eden between God who was unity and Satan, who was complexity, with no means of deciding which was truth."

China was on Henry Adams's mind. He predicted that the new century's heathenish meaning or meaninglessness might come to focus there. He wrote, in *The Education*: "The drama acted in Peking, in the summer of 1900, was, in the eyes of the student [that is, himself], the most serious that could be offered for his study, since it brought him suddenly to the inevitable struggle for the control of China, which, in his view, must decide the control of the world."

c/s

It was in the moment of that struggle, with so much history in store, that the little boy Henry Luce got whisked away from the shores of China, on a gunboat, out into the Yellow Sea. He was rescued in the nick of time—or "in time's nick," as his newsmagazine would have phrased it later on.

So it was that Harry Luce embarked upon the twentieth century.

c/s

After the Boxers subsided, the Luces returned and resumed their work of building the Kingdom of God on the other side of the world from Scranton, Pennsylvania. Now, after the rebellion's suppression, the Chinese became elaborately polite and submissive, for they had seen the foreigners' armies and their power. They had only to wait, however—for the end of the Manchu dynasty and the coming of Sun Yat-sen and then the warlords' time, and after that, Chiang and Mao and the Japanese; all the evolutions of the complicated twentieth century. China was not the same after the summer of 1900.

Henry R. Luce was conceived on a steamer somewhere on the Pacific, between San Francisco and Yokohama, on his missionary parents' honeymoon voyage to the mission field on the other side of the world. Little Harry spent the formative years of his life, from the ages of two to twelve, in that interval of China's false submission to the foreigners, between the Boxer Rebellion in 1900 and the formation of Sun Yat-sen's republic in 1911, when Harry, aged thirteen, was shipped off to Hotchkiss as a scholarship student. It is possible that his sometimes-misguided impressions of China emerged from that period when he was Little Boy Luce, princeling and prodigy at the mission compound, preaching Bible texts to the servants' children in imitation of his admirable blue-eyed father, the Reverend Henry Winters Luce, in whose study long-robed Chinese scholars gathered daily to discuss the New Testament and China's future as a Christian land.

☙

Luce used the word "selah" sometimes—in his letters, for example, as he signed off. A somewhat mysterious word, "selah" appears seventy-four times in the Hebrew Bible—sixty-nine times in the Psalms. As: "O Lord, how many are my foes! Many are rising against me; many are saying of my soul, there is no salvation for him in God. Selah" (Psalms 3:1–2). The word is said to be untranslatable—perhaps a musical notation, or else a sort of exclamation meaning, roughly, Take heed! Think! Stop! Reflect! Think calmly about this.

Hunter S. Thompson, who did not seem to think calmly about anything, used the word often in his letters and diaries—but he did it as a satirical affectation, in the spirit of, say, H.L. Mencken, who liked to razz the Bible Belt. Both Thompson and Luce were gonzo journalists. Thompson was cool and Luce was square. Thompson worked with styles of dire prophecy that were interbraided with burlesque.

Luce used the word "selah" a bit as he used the phrase "light and leading"—a gesture of his prophetic earnestness done up in a glancing, half-humorous reference to his missionary boyhood. He colored the thought with a slight, deft mockery of his own earnestness. He told his editors, with a wry smile, "Our readers may need light and leading on this point."

Yet he seemed to mean "selah" as the psalmist meant it: Take heed.

It is a useful word—an interactive word: The writer gives stage directions to the reader's mind. ∎

CHAPTER 21

Many claimed that John Hersey's 60,000-word report on the aftermath of the Hiroshima bombing—first published as the entire contents of a special issue of the *New Yorker* in August 1946, one year after the bomb fell—was the greatest work of journalism in the twentieth century.

If Hersey's journalism was the century's best, what was the worst?

As I have mentioned, it was arguably Walter Duranty's 1932 performance in the *New York Times*, a series of articles that he wrote in praise of Joseph Stalin just when Stalin was deliberately starving to death millions of people in Ukraine and the North Caucasus and the Lower Volga and other agricultural regions of the Soviet Union. Stalin seemed content with his own rationale: He needed to collectivize the farms, because he needed the grain for foreign exchange and to feed the workers in the factories with which the Soviet Union desperately needed to industrialize, rapidly, so that it might become a great power before another world war came along (as Stalin foresaw it would), in which the Germans might invade and overwhelm the Soviet Union. The farmers—the "kulaks," an invidious term that suggested bourgeois selfishness and greed—resisted collectivization. Stalin hadn't the time or patience to persuade them. He took their grain away from them and presently millions of them died of starvation.

&

Hersey and Duranty, I suppose, fit nicely into a theological interpretation of journalism, for they were saint and devil.

Duranty, an Englishman, graduate of Harrow and Cambridge, became a disciple and longtime friend of the somewhat tacky, threadbare Satanist Aleister Crowley, who called himself Beast 666, practiced "magick," and claimed to be "the wickedest man in the world." In Paris, where Duranty lived for some time as a penniless but resourceful bohemian in the years before World War I, Duranty and Crowley shared a mistress and now and then organized sex orgies tricked up as Satanist rituals—black masses sometimes, in which the "communion" was Duranty's sperm. Duranty was at times addicted to opium, which he adored.

And yet, astonishingly, starting as a stringer and then as a correspondent for the *New York Times* in the Great War, he became an extraordinarily accomplished journalist, fast, thorough, with a dramatic flair. Before long, he was possibly the best-known newspaperman in the world. In the 1920s, a train accident caused him to lose part of his left leg, so that he walked with a limp and a cane, with which he gestured flamboyantly. He was a small and apparently unprepossessing man, and the limp and cane did nothing to diminish the impression of him as a vaguely sinister figure. But he had very bright eyes and a gift of conversation, and, for one reason or another, he was very attractive to women.

John Hersey, a generation younger, was the anti-Duranty. He was a golden boy of America's WASP ascendancy—a tall, athletic, handsome, round-faced Boy Scout of a man with a muscular neck, a decisive, energetic, innocent mind, and a direct gaze and a natural gift of words. In 1943 when Hersey applied to join the navy, Hotchkiss sent a testimonial that said he represented "all that is best in the young manhood of America."

Like Henry Luce, Hersey was the son of China missionaries. Like Luce, he had graduated from Hotchkiss and Yale and had made Skull and Bones. He had become Luce's protégé at Time Inc. Luce thought of him as a possible successor as editor-in-chief. Once or twice, Luce offered Hersey the kingdom, at one point sending him this pompous telegram:

> The time has come when we must take definite decisions regarding
> the future of time the newsmagazine accordingly in my judgment
> you should begin work as a senior editor of Time not later than
> January first stop for three reasons first in order to participate in the
> creative planning of postwar time second to learn the art and trade of
> being an editor third because we are in serious need of a competent
> senior editor.

Hersey's 60,000-word report on the aftermath of Hiroshima became a defining work of American journalism. It was taken to be journalism as an act of witness and even of love—and indeed an indirect declaration of American shame and a sort of apology (even if most Americans were perfectly content with the Hiroshima and Nagasaki bombs that ended the war).

ᴄ⋄ɔ

I have tried, from time to time over the years, to write essays about Hiroshima and have fussed over the arguments, the pros and cons.

Were the atom bombs on Hiroshima and Nagasaki a blessing or a curse? They had saved lives, people claimed and continue to claim, and they hastened the end of the long and terrible war. They averted the need for an invasion of the Japanese home islands. They had of course taken many lives, as well—and done so horribly enough.

The poet Robert Lowell years later would write a line in regard to Vietnam: "My eyes have seen what my hand has done." Hersey minutely examined what the American hand had done at Hiroshima.

There are few journalist saints. Woodward and Bernstein were hardly saints but rather, at most, knights-errant, exemplars in a lesser, political/criminal theater of war. In the usual allegory of Watergate, Youth (Woodward and Bernstein) rose out of obscurity (doing menial reporting jobs at the *Washington Post*) to chastise the Corruption of the Elders (Nixon et al., the authors not only of Watergate but also of Vietnam, of everything that had gone Bad and Rotten in America, as disclosed in that great transformation, the decade that began with Kennedy's assassination and ended with Watergate).

Hersey's *Hiroshima* was a different thing: a work of atonement—a spiritual document, a reckoning, an elegy. A sort of confession. It had about it an immaculate clarity and dispassion and a validating, underlying grief. Watergate was one of the twentieth century's history plays; Hiroshima was a tragedy. The youthful Hersey undertook to grasp the event by means of the simplest, most straightforward journalism. He went to Hiroshima and interviewed people for six weeks and came home and wrote it up in transparent prose: not an ounce of fat or rhetoric. It was a lesson in egoless narrative. It might be seen as a premonitory rebuke of the New Journalism that was to come, which, at its worst, became a carnival of self-indulgence or the performance of children playing moral dress-up and making themselves the stars of their histories: The greatest egoless American prose style, I suppose, was that of Abraham Lincoln, whose work, like Hersey's, had the mystic underpinning of grief.

World War II saw many innovations in the science and technology of mass death, including Auschwitz and Treblinka. The Soviet Russians lost twenty million in their Great Patriotic War. Stalin's Great Famine in Ukraine and the North Caucasus and elsewhere, along with his terror and gulag (the Great Fear) killed at least twenty million more of his own people.

Human ingenuity had found a way to diddle the minuscule atom (the closest thing in the universe to nothing at all) and, in that diddling, to destroy an entire city—with promise of infinitely more destruction to come. *Kamikaze* meant "divine wind" in Japanese; that was mere samurai poetry: bravado. It was the Americans who conjured the truly divine or satanic wind. They dropped it like a little seed out of a clear summer morning, and it fell to earth and blossomed.

"As Mrs. Nakamura stood watching her neighbor," John Hersey reported, "everything flashed whiter than any white she had ever seen . . . something picked her up and she seemed to fly into the next room over the raised sleeping platform, pursued by parts of her house."

In a city of 250,000, Hersey wrote, "nearly a hundred thousand people had been killed or doomed at one blow; a hundred thousand more were hurt."

And so that was part of it—the sheer suddenness and unnatural speed of the annihilation.

Hersey told the stories, moment to moment, of six people (including a German Jesuit who had lived and worked among the people of the city for years) upon whom the bomb had fallen. The story amounted entirely to a narrative of witness. Hersey's storytelling clarity—the purest journalistic objectivity—accommodated itself to the surreal and unprecedented event: "Houses nearby were burning, and when huge drops of water the size of marbles began to fall, he half thought that they must be coming from the hoses of firemen fighting the blazes. (They were actually drops of condensed moisture falling from the turbulent tower of dust, heat, and fission fragments that had already risen miles into the sky above Hiroshima.)"

The universe started all over again, traveling, it seemed, in the wrong direction. Hiroshima was the new Big Bang—instead of representing the Creation, it foretold the incipient Extinction.

The power of Hersey's *Hiroshima* emerged in part from his grasp of the resonances, an air of deepest sadness and elegy. Hersey came to report not the Good News but the Bad News—in essence, another Fall of Man. But Hersey's account had the defect of its own simplicity. There was much more to be said about the bombing of Hiroshima. Hersey's act of contrition seems, on reflection, to be morally incomplete and even a little fatuous.

The meaning of Hiroshima lay neither in the number of people killed by the bomb nor in the unusual nature of their suffering. Rather, it was to be found in the apocalyptic implication of the weapon—one black-clad gun-type uranium fission bomb, the size of a big hot-water heater—that dropped out of the *Enola Gay* and destroyed the city of Hiroshima and (now that the secret was out and about) might, sometime in the future and perhaps pretty soon, destroy the world itself. The bomb was Pandora's Box.

The meaning lay in the limitless physics of chain reaction—war not as conquest (a comparatively trivial thing that might in a decade or a century be undone) but as obliteration. It might extinguish time itself. Both world wars had flirted with such ideas—at places like the Somme and in other great slaughters of the First World War, and after that, in the indiscriminate bombings of Dresden and Hamburg or in the siege of Stalingrad.

ℭℌ

How to think about these things? Was it the job of journalists such as Hersey to think about them and weigh them from a moral point of view? The mind sought out grounds of comparison. The American fire-bombings of Tokyo in the spring of 1945 had killed as many or more people than "Little Boy" at Hiroshima—and had killed them just as horribly. Tokyo was a city made of wood and paper; General Curtis LeMay's incendiary bombs created an inferno fully as annihilating and hellish as the one that flattened Hiroshima.

If Hersey had gone to Nanking months after the Japanese army had perpetrated the Rape of Nanking, in late 1937 and early 1938—involving the rape of some 80,000 women and girls and the killing of as many as 300,000 Chinese (three times the number of Japanese killed by the bomb at Hiroshima)—and if he had recorded the stories, in detail, of Chinese people who had been there and whose families had been brutalized in the six-week-long rampage, then he might have written a book just as vivid and indelible. And, incidentally, such a book would have acted to mute, somewhat, the effect of his Hiroshima account, since it would be thought, in an informal way (as many people thought at the time), that Hiroshima was in part merely payback for the Rape of Nanking and Bataan and Manila and other heinous Japanese atrocities. The Japanese Rape of Nanking (unlike the atom bomb dropped on Hiroshima) was not a military operation that had a sound if arguable rationale and that might be defended as a way of ultimately saving lives and bringing a long, destructive war to an end; the Rape of Nanking was an act of collective bestiality, committed over a protracted period of time—a long drama of thousands of individual acts of unthinkable viciousness.

A book by Hersey recording the Japanese army's behavior in minute and vivid detail would also have had its effect. If, just after the war, he had written not about Hiroshima but about Nanking, the book might have had the effect of causing the American occupation of Japan to be brutal and punitive, instead of mild, as it was. It might have inflamed feelings of hatred against the Japanese for a generation or two.

☙

Again, the difference at Hiroshima was the novelty and the terrifying power of that one bomb—and the fact that it was only one. And yet the Japanese behavior at Nanking was also terrifying. Nanking—like

Auschwitz, like Pol Pot's Killing Fields, though all the cases are different—disclosed unthinkably evil potential in the hearts of ordinary human beings.

Once one has grasped the principles of the atom bomb and has overcome initial surprise that so small a weapon could accomplish so much destruction, it becomes, over time, an objective military and political fact in the world—lamentable and ominous but eventually familiar. Truman's decision to drop the bomb was not a mystery; one may quarrel with his reasoning, and with the necessity of the bomb, but his rationale was clear and defensible, not only on military but even on moral grounds (saving lives, both American and Japanese, that would have been lost in an invasion of the home islands). One also acknowledges, uneasily, the argument that the Japanese were finished, in any case—their resources (oil, etc.) exhausted—and that Truman might simply have waited, resisting the temptation to deliver the decisive, apocalyptic blow.

A number of countries possess nuclear arsenals now. They are an evolution in a bad direction, a threat to the future of the world; but they are no longer what one would call either a mystery or a novelty. Their existence makes the future of the world more of a mystery than it would be otherwise, but that is a different thing.

Iris Chang's *The Rape of Nanking* documented the extraordinary evil done by ordinary Japanese soldiers. She wrote:

> Many soldiers went beyond rape to disembowel women, slice off their breasts, nail them alive to walls. Fathers were forced to rape their daughters, and sons their mothers, as other family members watched. Not only did live burials, castration, the carving of organs and the roasting of people become routine, but more diabolical tortures were practiced, such as hanging people by their tongues on iron hooks or burying people to their waists and watching them torn apart by German shepherds. So sickening was the spectacle that even Nazis in the city were horrified.

To a normal mind, such behavior remains inexplicable. Iris Chang was a Chinese American journalist. Her book became an instant best seller; but, published in 1997, sixty years after the massacre happened, it did not create the popular sensation that Hersey's did. Chang was working on a book about the Bataan Death March—another episode of extreme Japanese barbarity—at the time she committed suicide in 2004 at the age of thirty-six. She shot herself on a country road in California; she left behind suicide notes. She suffered from depression, and I suppose it is possible that she might have killed herself even if she'd had perfectly cheerful work—say, as the garden columnist of the *Sacramento Bee*. But one can guess that her subject matter (Nanking, Bataan, the mystery of such evil behavior) may have overwhelmed her.

Another difference between Hiroshima and Nanking: The American bomb dropped on Hiroshima was the work of remarkably few—scientists and workers at Los Alamos, military officers. The decision that the greatest democracy in the world would use the bomb was made ultimately by only one man, Harry Truman. It was top-down evil, so to speak, if you think of Hiroshima as evil. Nanking, on the other hand, seems to have emerged from the vicious impulses of the men themselves and of young officers (two of whom held an infamous competition to see which of them, using a samurai sword, could behead one hundred Chinese in the shorter time). The evil at Nanking had a disturbing spontaneity about it. War had cracked open the id, and Nanking was the result. Whatever else one may say about the atom bomb, it was hardly a spontaneous or, as it were, democratic act.

But Elie Wiesel warned against comparing one evil to another. Each evil is unique and, like Agassiz's fish, should be examined on its own terms.

છ

Most Americans rejoiced that Harry Truman had dropped the bomb, on the commonsense, Curtis LeMay logic that war is horrible, and you should get it over with quickly and brutally; this war had gone on for years, with ever-growing accumulations of bodies and with ever-rising levels of savagery and inhumanity.

Every president at one time or another disliked or feared Henry Luce. One evening after the war, Harry Truman confronted Luce at a Washington function (a *Newsweek* cocktail party, of all things) and barked at him, "I don't know how you can sleep at night, printing the things that you do!" I thought of that scene in the context of Hiroshima, because it was Truman who later said that after he made the decision to bomb Hiroshima, he went upstairs in the White House and got a good night's sleep.

There was another story, this one involving J. Robert Oppenheimer, who visited Truman in the Oval Office several years after Hiroshima and told him, in some anguish, "I feel as if I have blood on my hands." Truman is said to have responded by offering him his handkerchief and saying, scornfully, "Here, wipe it off!"

I used to think that the great American themes—the binaries—were Success and Failure. Now I think that, more deeply, the themes are Innocence and Guilt.

(What else is the great American theme of race all about?)

☙

At the time of Hiroshima, the author William Manchester was on a troop ship on his way across the Pacific with thousands of other American young men being assembled for a final assault on the Japanese home islands. Some estimates said that as many as 500,000 of those men would have died in such an invasion; Japanese resistance might be expected to be as fanatical as it had been on Okinawa, in April, when 48,000 Americans were killed or wounded taking the island. Many Okinawans had killed themselves, jumping off high cliffs rather than surrender to the Americans, whose occupation promised dishonor and something worse than death. Manchester and the other young men there considered that the attack on Hiroshima had saved their lives.

Hersey wrote on a moral plane that rose above the merely strategic. He insisted, in prose suffused with sorrow and indignation and the implication of deeper principle, upon the superseding humanity of those upon whom the bomb had fallen. The infliction of such suffering must itself be evil.

Hersey's moral technique was subtle. In a painstaking, intricate tapestry of detail, he turned the Japanese victims into human beings—actual and suffering. Hersey called his characters "Mr. Nakamura" or "Dr. Sasaki," using titles of respect. He accumulated details that made their lives human and ordinary and sympathetic, only superficially different from the lives of Americans in Wichita or Oskaloosa. He recorded their terrible suffering on that morning and after and their occasional heroism. Theirs were lives that—except for the world-historical tragedy—might have appeared in a story in the *Saturday Evening Post*.

Even before the publication of *Hiroshima*, Hersey was fairly famous as a war correspondent and best-selling author. His novel *A Bell for Adano* had won the Pulitzer Prize in 1945. It was about a fictional Italian town in the middle of World War II, which an American army major named Joppolo attempts to return to decency and honor after the Allies have driven out the Fascist regime. Henry Luce had sent Hersey as a *Time-Life* correspondent in Italy after he had covered the battle for Guadalcanal—and written a creditable book about it called *Into the Valley*. ∎

CHAPTER 22

Hersey and Luce, though remarkably similar in some ways, were, in essence, opposites. The difference had to do with their attitudes toward power. Luce admired power—feared it, respected it, understood it—and rejoiced in its possibilities as an agent of Good and God. Hersey mistrusted power and saw the tragedy and suffering that power visited upon people. His rejection of Luce's offer to put him in charge of the entire *Time-Life* empire someday was the clearest demonstration of what made each man tick. Hersey did not want the power; he was appalled by it. I suspect that Luce found his attitude incomprehensible.

Luce traveled the world, talking to presidents, foreign ministers, dictators, autocrats, corporate heads. They accepted him as one of their own. He ran an empire of information, journalism, entertainment. When he returned to the New York office—the citadel of the Time-Life Building in Rockefeller Center—he wrote memos to his editors about the state of the world. He told them about it at a hundred lunches with his managing editors—his College of Cardinals. He understood the responsibilities and temptations of power; he sympathized with the powerful; he judged generals and presidents and dictators by what they did with their power, how they used it for (in *Time*'s portentous phrase) "good or ill."

Luce's deepest convictions revolved around the dilemmas and temptations of power. God was all-powerful, and Luce, like John Milton, sought to justify the ways of God to men. Luce knew God meant that power should be used for good—the advancement of freedom, of Christianity, of capitalism (all of those things being good in his eyes and adding up, more or less, in some optative dimension of the world that he thought of as the Kingdom of God). His great preoccupation was with the moral exercise of power. If power was used for bad purposes, that meant it was either satanic or stupid—and in either case, must be reproved. After World War II, he asked repeatedly: What should America do with its great power in the world? What should America do with an "American century" that had been bestowed upon the country by history? Power must stand for something—it will either be evil and venal and corrupt, or it will be constructive, in the way that his father and the other missionaries of his childhood had been constructive, building schools, colleges, hospitals.

But, for a follower of Christ, Luce's heart was somewhat cold. He had little instinct for the victims or the little people. He did not spend time among them or ask them questions about themselves. Their lives, I suspect, did not quite interest him. (That was what Pearl Buck hated about him.)

He was focused upon his idea of America as a great thing in the world—as a doer, a God-sponsored winner, a force. He sentimental-ized small-town America (in the way of Thornton Wilder or Norman Rockwell), but he lavished his great editorial love (to put it that way) or, anyway, his admiration upon powerful corporations, powerful industrial-ists, powerful ideas, powerful deeds, powerful accomplishments. Virtuous power, in his theology, would naturally see to the welfare of the powerless, although, as a matter of doctrine, he did not like to concede that any American was "powerless." The powerless did not seem to interest him much. It was a flaw in him—a missing circuit.

His instinct—like Benjamin Franklin's—was entrepreneurial: the American dynamic. He expected of each individual a mighty, consci-entious striving. He thought of America as a kind of god, or as God's favorite idea.

Harry Luce did not like the condescension—the spiritual insult, the solecism—implicit in moaning over the sufferings of others. The Calvinist soul must work out its own destiny. In all this, again, he was like John Bunyan's Christian in *The Pilgrim's Progress*—gruff, straightforward, uncompromising, intolerant of weakness and self-pity. His models of virtue were less Christian than Roman or Greek.

He was, on the other hand, sympathetic to the plight of American blacks and to the struggle for civil rights. He knew injustice when he saw it. But to him America was an exalted project, the great power on the side of good. America was too tremendous, too good, to make an obsession of the suffering poor—and there lurked in such thinking (in sentimentality) the hazard of totalitarianism. He had seen the dangers of other great powers of the earth—Nazism, Communism—and who can blame him for being preoccupied by the problem of how to keep such wicked powers, manipulating the masses, from prevailing?

John Hersey tended—as Luce did not—to see the evil within: He thought of Hiroshima as a supreme abuse of American power, as well as the culmination, as it were, of all the bad tendencies of mankind since the Garden. It was a great sin.

Luce trained in 1918 at the army camp at Plattsburgh, New York, but the Great War ended before he could make it to Europe to join in the fighting. During World War II, President Roosevelt mostly prevented Luce (and other publishers) from visiting battle zones. (His wife Clare did serve for a time as a first-class war correspondent in Italy and elsewhere for *Life*.) So Luce was never close to war or to the soldiers fighting. His correspondents did a mostly brilliant job of covering the troops, the battles. Luce was frustrated by Roosevelt's vindictive policy that kept him out of war zones and had to be content with being a Big Picture editor, seeing the war through his proxies, including Hersey. His war, in this one sense, was like that of General George C. Marshall, whom Roosevelt kept in Washington to mastermind the global effort. Marshall had badly wanted to go overseas and command troops, but he stayed in the capital, as the president wished, and fulfilled his assignment nobly.

Hersey was not a Communist, but he was myopic or astigmatic where Communism was concerned. Stalin and Mao over the course of many years proved there was, to say the least, good reason to oppose Communism. Accounts of the history of *Time* and Luce in those years— e.g., of the rebellion, just after the war, of certain left-leaning correspondents for the magazine (Charles Wertenbaker and John Osborne and John Hersey and Walter Graebner, among others) against foreign editor and apostate Communist Whittaker Chambers—make out the correspondents to be the good guys and Luce and Chambers to be reactionary Republicans and totally in the wrong. But it was the correspondents who were essentially wrong about Stalin and Communist rule.

Luce abhorred "Dr. New Deal"—FDR in the 1930s—as a failure; but after Pearl Harbor, he ardently supported "Dr. Win-the-War" as a great success. When Roosevelt died in 1945, Luce said, "I suppose it is my duty to go on hating him." It was one of the more complex things he ever said. It was not a line to be taken at face value.

Franklin Roosevelt was a mysterious man. So was Henry Luce—mysterious with an explanation. The two men were variations on the theme of unreadable character. Even Roosevelt's closest friends and allies felt, at one time or another, deceived and baffled by FDR; most of them eventually settled for the conclusion reached by his adoring speechwriter, the playwright Robert Sherwood, who wrote that Roosevelt was an indecipherable mystery, "multiplex, contradictory to a bewildering degree." Roosevelt's mind, wrote Sherwood, was an impenetrable and "heavily forested interior."

Roosevelt acknowledged himself—proudly, slyly—to be an actor. He told Orson Welles that the two of them were the greatest actors in America. Roosevelt's polio obliged him to become a master of deception—on important public occasions, he *seemed* to walk, even though he floated a fraction of an inch above the floor, supported on either side by one of his big sons or by a muscular Secret Service man. Roosevelt made the curious boast that sometimes his left hand was engaged in activities of which his right hand was innocent and unaware.

Luce knew exactly what each hand was doing (in his case, the two hands were church and state). He never *acted*, never pretended, never performed. He was incapable of it. He never played any part except that of Harry Luce. He thought of acting (by a politician) as a form of lying and hypocrisy. The truth had no need to lie. Roosevelt was Shakespeare's Prospero and Luce was John Bunyan's Christian.

And yet Luce had a boyish attraction to such flamboyant performers as Douglas MacArthur, one of the stagiest characters in the Age of Luce, and to Winston Churchill, who rehearsed his grandiloquent speeches in front of a mirror. Luce liked heroes and adventure stories. Some part of his character remained about fourteen years old. ■

CHAPTER 23

Luce was a spiritual and journalistic descendant of Cotton Mather, whose *Magnalia Christi Americana* (*The Glorious Works of Christ in America*), published in 1702, had a rambling, magazine feel about it. Luce's magazines were equally the descendants of William McGuffey, who invented the McGuffey Readers that tutored generations of nineteenth-century Americans, especially out in the heartland. Henry Ford, who did something to invent the twentieth century, and who had hated the life on the Michigan farm where he spent his nineteenth-century boyhood, nevertheless had an overwhelming nostalgia for McGuffey Readers, collecting them by the thousands and installing them in his museum in Dearborn.

There was also in Luce, for all of his life, a corny, unembarrassed vein of Henry Wadsworth Longfellow and his "Psalm of Life":

What the Heart of the Young Man Said to the Psalmist.
. . .
Life is real! Life is earnest!
And the grave is not its goal.
. . .
. . .
Not enjoyment, and not sorrow,
Is our destined end or way;
But to act, that each tomorrow
Find us farther than today.
. . .
Act, and act in the living Present!
Heart within and God o'erhead!

> Lives of great men all remind us
> We can make our lives sublime,
> And, departing, leave behind us,
> Footprints in the sands of time.

Time cover stories told the lives of "great men" and great villains sometimes; their lives left footprints in the pages of *Time* and the minds of its readers. The nineteenth century thought of history as something heroic and personalized—"the history of living men." That was Luce's idea as well, and his journalism sought to present a living record of men and women in the act of making history.

> Let us, then, be up and doing,
> With a heart for any fate;
> Still achieving, still pursuing,
> Learn to labor, and to wait.

Longfellow's poem was published in 1835. What were those thoughts but an almost formal agenda for the nineteenth century? *Be up and doing!* That was the "pep," the "Lucepower," of the Reverend Henry Winters Luce. In his son Harry a century later (in 1935, in the heart of the Great Depression), there was none of the futility and despair and cynicism and bafflement of Modernism. That was one of the reasons for his magazines' success.

୧୨

Luce was related, by inclination, to George Bancroft, the nineteenth-century historian whose heroic ten-volume history of the United States amounted to an American *Aeneid*. Later schools of historians derided Bancroft as being more mythologist and epic poet than serious scholar. That much was true.

George Bancroft was born in the fall of 1800, a year after the death of George Washington. He died in the winter of 1891, seven years before the birth of Henry Luce.

Bancroft's ancestors arrived in Massachusetts in the 1630s around the same time that the original American Henry Luce came to Martha's Vineyard. Both the early Bancrofts and the early Luces were sturdy farmers and Calvinists. George Bancroft's father went to Harvard and became a Congregational minister. Henry Luce's father went to Yale and became a Presbyterian minister and missionary.

When I say that Henry Luce was a nineteenth-century man, I have in mind the American nineteenth century of George Bancroft—not only the idealized America that Bancroft the historian created in his *History of the United States of America* but also the America of Bancroft the diplomat and public servant. As secretary of the navy under James K. Polk, Bancroft created the US Naval Academy at Annapolis. (He also abolished flogging in the navy.) He served as US minister to London and to Berlin. He was, like Luce, an international man, whose friends included Macaulay, Carlyle, and Bismarck. He was born into the new America of Washington and Jefferson, and "his life spanned more than three-quarters of the independent existence of the nation whose history he wrote, and of which he was a part," commented the historian Russell B. Nye, who edited an edition of the Bancroft history. "The public expected history to be presented as a dramatic conflict of opposing individuals, forces or nations; the historian, like the playwright, imposed form and structure on the disorder of events, finding tension, climax, and resolution in the segments of human experience he chose to write about." That approach had much to do with Luce's journalistic practice.

Nye remarked, "To Bancroft, American history from 1492 to 1789 was a continuous, unified narrative of how a divinely favored people found the meaning of freedom, fought for it in a bitter contest against Old World Tyranny, and in the American system of constitutional union fashioned the perfect instrument for its preservation."

To Bancroft, a Jacksonian Democrat, equality was as prominent a value as freedom. "Jacksonian" would become a loaded, binary word later on—implying not merely the broadening base of inclusive democracy as the voice of new people from beyond the Appalachians asserted itself, but also, on its dark side, the genocidal violence of Andrew Jackson's Trail of Tears, the expulsion of the Cherokee, and, by extension, all of the criminal ruthlessness of the white Europeans' settlement of North America.

But Bancroft was concerned with the Enlightenment refulgence of the tale:

> The United States of America constitute an essential portion of a great political system, embracing all the civilized nations of the earth. At a period when the force of moral opinion is rapidly increasing, they have the precedence in the practice and the defense of the equal rights of man.
>
> The sovereignty of the people is here a conceded axiom, and the laws, established upon that basis, are cherished with faithful patriotism...Prosperity follows the execution of even justice; invention is quickened by the freedom of competition; and labor rewarded with sure and unexampled returns.

Bancroft's vision of America helped to formalize that self-image of innocence—almost of immaculate conception, a sort of incipient Kingdom of God—that would become the object of Graham Greene's scorn in the 1950s, when the CIA was busy in the world. Bancroft conjured an idyllic America before the Civil War, before the Gilded Age, before the robber barons and their rapacities, before mass immigration, urbanization, massive industrialization and the labor troubles marked by the violence of Haymarket and Ludlow, the rise of class warfare, Populism, Wobblies—the polarizing complexities that would serve to discredit and all but sink Bancroft's naive version of America.

A vein of the country's thinking—and of Harry Luce's—dreamed of what Van Wyck Brooks called "a usable past." Was there such a thing? (Lincoln's appeal to "the mystic chords of memory" did not prevent the Civil War; those memories were not, so to speak, usable.) And how would one "use" such a past? As inspiration? As a model? As self-delusion? As a deep keel in rough seas?

Would America have a "usable future"? Americans generally assumed that the future, through technological progress, would yield ever more useful tools that would in turn lead the country on into new dimensions of possibility and progress. And it often happened that way.

Luce in his magazines picked up these American themes and tried to negotiate the discrepancy between the country's mythic and ideal (Bancroft) dimension, on the one hand, and, on the other hand, its hard and carefully reported realities. His journalism was sometimes highly colored.

A Bancroft sampler:

"A gallant navy protects our commerce ... while we avoid entangling participation in [foreign powers'] intrigues, their passions, and their wars."

"Every man may enjoy the fruits of his industry; every mind is free to publish its convictions."

"Even the enemies of the state, if there are any among us, have liberty to express their opinions undisturbed."

"New states are forming in the wilderness ... manufactures prosper ... the use of steam on our rivers and railroads annihilates distance by the acceleration of speed."

"There is no national debt; the community is opulent; the government economical; and the public treasury full."

Before the white men came to the New World:

"The whole territory was an unproductive waste ... Its only inhabitants were a few scattered tribes of feeble barbarians, destitute of commerce and of political connection. The axe and the ploughshare were unknown. The soil ... was lavishing its strength in magnificent but useless vegetation. In the view of civilization, the immense domain (America) was a solitude.

"It is the object of the present work to explain how the change in the condition of our land has been brought about; and, as the fortunes of a nation are not under the control of blind destiny, to follow the steps by which a favoring Providence, calling our institutions into being, has conducted the country to its present happiness and glory."

Later generations would judge the Bancroft version to be delusional and odious and even monstrous (racist, white supremacist, and all that)—unforgivable. But Luce, if he could, would protest, "No, you don't understand. That wasn't it at all." Bancroft and Luce thought of America as a work in progress, the evolving Kingdom of God. Their idealized vision of America, I think, was not hypocrisy but something else—a kind of yearning, an Emersonian idealism. There was even an innocence in it.

In 1898, just about the time Henry Luce was born in Shandong, a fervent young Republican named Albert Beveridge was running for the Senate in Indiana. America was just launching itself into the world by intervening in Cuba, in what became the Spanish-American War. Beveridge caught the imperial moment exactly in one of his campaign speeches: "Fellow-citizens—It is a noble land that God has given us; a land that can feed and clothe the world; a land whose coast lines would enclose half the countries of Europe; a land set like a sentinel between the two imperial oceans of the globe; a greater England with a nobler destiny. It is a mighty people that He has planted on this soil; a people sprung from the most masterful blood of history." It was American Kipling, no doubt. And that phrase, "masterful blood," indicts it. But the moment passed. Beveridge, along with Theodore Roosevelt, would eventually move considerably to the left of their own imperialist rhetoric. They even began to sound almost like Socialists.

Luce's article called "The American Century" was published in *Life* in February 1941—nine months before Pearl Harbor. Luce had two purposes: to urge Americans to get directly involved in the defense of Britain against Hitler; and to persuade them that they must, in the long term, replace Great Britain as the preeminent power in a changed international system. The American left misconstrued the article and called it a typical piece of Lucean arrogance. Vice President Henry Wallace wrote sanctimoniously that, rather than an American Century, he would prefer a "Century of the Common Man."

The fuss over the "American Century" piece was a good example of the unfairness and even the stupidity of the doctrinaire left's dismissal of Luce. He was correct on both his points. Something about Luce drove the left crazy, but history often proved him to be right.

☙

In the spring of 1966, *Life* published an article about Allen Ginsberg and his poetry. The author of the piece, a young *Life* writer named Barry Farrell, claimed that Ginsberg might be America's new Walt Whitman. The comparison infuriated Luce, to whom Whitman's *Leaves of Grass* was a sacred American text, a life-vision of the country. Ginsberg's poem "Howl" seemed to Luce a death-vision—and awful poetry besides.

On October 17, 1954, Allen Ginsberg took peyote in his apartment at 755 Pine Street in San Francisco, and he had a vision in which the Sir Francis Drake Hotel and the Medical Arts Building were transformed into the image of the ancient Phoenician god Moloch. Ten months later, Ginsberg began to write a poem, based on the Moloch vision, that he first called "Strophes" and later renamed "Howl." It began:

> I saw the best minds of my generation destroyed by madness,
>   starving hysterical naked, dragging themselves through the
>   negro streets at dawn looking for an angry fix,
> angelheaded hipsters burning for the ancient heavenly connection to
>   the starry dynamo in the machinery of night,
> who poverty and tatters and hollow-eyed and high sat up smoking in
>   the supernatural darkness of cold-water flats floating across the
>   tops of cities contemplating jazz,
> who bared their brains to Heaven under the El and saw
>   Mohammedan angels staggering on tenement roofs illuminated,
> who passed through universities with radiant cool eyes hallucinating
>   Arkansas and Blake-light tragedy among the scholars of war,
> who were expelled from the academies for crazy & publishing
>   obscene odes on the windows of the skull,
> who cowered in unshaven rooms in underwear, burning their money
>   in wastebaskets and listening to the Terror through the wall,
> who got busted in their public beards returning through Laredo with
>   a belt of marijuana for New York,
> who ate fire in paint hotels or drank turpentine in Paradise Alley,
>   death, or purgatoried their torsos night after night
> with dreams, with drugs, with waking nightmares, alcohol and cock
>   and endless balls.

"Howl" and Jack Kerouac's *On the Road*, the Beat Generation's principal texts, were published in 1957 and prepared the way for the 1960s. They became part of the underground folklore that attacked the Eisenhower time and its perceived conformities and hypocrisies. Ginsberg wrote another poem, called "Laughing Gas," that repeated the idea:

Today apocalypse
  Tomorrow
Mickey Mouse cartoons.

I'm disgusted! It's unbelievable!
How could it all be so
    Horrible and funny?
      It's a dirty joke!
The whole universe a shaggy dog story.

Now, twelve years later, Luce expressed his indignation a short time after Farrell's piece was published, on the night of the Hunt Ball, which was *Life* magazine's lavish annual party for its staff—dinner and dancing and much wine in the ballroom of the Plaza Hotel. It was the thirtieth anniversary of the founding of *Life*, 1966, and so Luce came from Phoenix to attend, although he had retired as editor-in-chief.

On such occasions, Luce was usually amiable and polite and paternal. But the Ginsberg article had offended him. After greeting the staff and saying a few nice things, he started grumbling about Farrell's Ginsberg article. The founder said he was ashamed that such malignant nonsense—comparing Walt Whitman to Allen Ginsberg—should appear in *Life*.

Young Barry Farrell's face reddened in mounting anger as he listened to Luce's denunciation. He sought out Luce afterward and bitterly objected to what he'd said. Luce softened and tried to be collegial, but it did not work, so he quoted some lines of Whitman from memory and challenged Farrell: "Now you give me some Ginsberg poetry that even comes close to that!"

Pretty soon, Barry Farrell resigned from the staff of *Life* and moved to Paris.

❧

Years later, Luce's elder son, Hank, was seated at a Manhattan dinner party across the table from Allen Ginsberg. Each knew perfectly well who the other was, but they pretended not to.

Ginsberg asked, "What do you do?"

Hank Luce grumpily listed his title (head of the Henry Luce Foundation) and then ran through the list of corporate boards on which he sat.

He asked Ginsberg, "And what do you do?"

"I'm a poet."

"A poet, eh? Well, let's hear some."

Ginsberg, for the fun of it, replied by reciting a few graphic and incredibly obscene lines describing sadomasochistic homosexual sex, ending with the words, "And he screamed, not in pain, but in pleasure."

Hank Luce, a shambling, Br'er Bear of a man, stared straight ahead for a long moment, his arms folded across his chest, his eyes swimming behind his thick glasses—considering.

At last, he gave up trying for a witty reply and grunted, "Huh! That's poetry, eh?"

Ginsberg figured he'd had the last laugh on the Luces. The poet was a close friend of Leila Luce, Hank's wife (his third), a wonderful writer who was also a friend of mine. She told me the story about the dinner party merrily enough, and I laughed. I did not tell her that I, like Harry Luce, detested Allen Ginsberg's work. ■

CHAPTER 24

Henry Luce is buried beside the Cooper River, on the coast of South Carolina—buried, of all things, on the grounds of Mepkin Abbey, a Trappist monastery, next to Clare, and next to his mother-in-law. Clare put him there when he died—and put herself there as well, years later, in 1988, when her time came. The widow gets to choose the grave site for both. Another last laugh.

Their graves overlook the lowlands and swamps and onetime rice plantations of South Carolina. Waterbirds migrate through, above beds of reeds and bulrushes. The remains of hectic chain-smoking ex-Puritan Harry Luce lie in another dimension, in amniotic heat and damp, the world about him moving in prehistoric slow motion—the hidden current of the Cooper River, the sinuosities of alligators, water moccasins, seasons of the year. The monks' prayers rise with incense, clouds of birds.

The Trappists at the monastery earn their living by raising chickens—thousands of them. A partnership of Church and State: The monks supply eggs to the military bases that proliferated around Charleston, thanks to the patron saint of the district, the late Congressman Mendel Rivers, of Gumville, South Carolina, who was chairman of the House Armed Services Committee during the years of the Vietnam War.

The monks observe silence. The air overhead is disturbed from time to time by the screams of jet fighters or by the boom of gunnery practice from a nearby army base—a reminder of the time when Luce was a boy and the German army occupying Tsingtao fired practice rounds from the hills and little Harry could see them splash, far out in the Yellow Sea. Now God and Caesar preside over his grave.

The Luces' headstones are white panels of soft, luminous marble, and around them stand live oaks draped with Spanish moss, like the cobwebs in the room in the inn on the Luces' first night in China, after they had landed on the coast of Shandong, when Harry was in his mother's womb and the Reverend Luce sat up all night, keeping watch, anxious to protect his bride.

For a wintry Presbyterian/Calvinist whose people had landed long ago on the rocky coast of New England, lowland South Carolina seems an unlikely place to come to rest.

Harry and Clare are there because at one time, they had owned the plantation, Mepkin, that is now a monastery. Harry had bought Mepkin for Clare in the 1930s, when such spreads were going for bargain prices. She loved the neighborhood because her former lover Bernard Baruch had a plantation nearby, called Hobcaw, where she had often stayed. Clare and Baruch had a May-December affair. When she married Luce, their intimacy ceased. Baruch said, "The eagle does not share his mate." They remained friends. Harry rather liked Bernie.

Clare's daughter by her first marriage (to an alcoholic millionaire named George Brokaw, whom she divorced) loved Mepkin and came there for school vacations—loved it because she knew that at Mepkin she would have her busy mother more to herself. Her name was Anne. She was killed in a car accident in 1943, and Clare could no longer bear to come to Mepkin after that because it reminded her of her daughter and made her feel guilty that she had not spent more time with her. Clare sought solace as a convert to the Catholic Church, and in 1948, the Luces offered to donate Mepkin to the Cistercians (Trappists).

The monks, with their headquarters at the Abbey of Gethsemani in Kentucky, debated among themselves whether to open a satellite house in what seemed the inhospitable country of lowland South Carolina. The celebrated brother among them, the writer Thomas Merton, commented in his diary on March 24, 1948: "South Carolina... The more I think about it, the more it seems to me to add up to seven thousand acres of fever and snakes, but that cannot be true. Millionaires don't build houses in swamps."

Harry and Clare, when they bought the plantation, engaged the New York architect Edward Durell Stone to design new buildings for them in sleek modern style, with white concrete cube-shaped guest houses and other buildings that offended southern traditionalists in the neighborhood. Southern coastal damp and mildew and insects and rot exacted revenge upon the Yankees: Before many years the new Luce houses had fallen into ruin.

Merton acquiesced in the Father Abbot's decision to accept the gift of the plantation on behalf of the monks. But in his diary Merton conjured a nightmare of what life would be like at Mepkin: "Damp moss hangs from the trees, you can barely see ten feet through the miasmas of the swamp. Nearby I recognize the tree on which the local citizens lynched four of the other monks. All around me the water moccasins slither through the grass, and I wonder if I can't get a pair of high leather boots to keep the snakes from biting me on the legs. Is that moss on the branch of that tree, or is it another snake?"

When some of the other monks moved down to South Carolina to the old Luce place, Merton remained at the mother house in Kentucky. He was a privileged character there, the famous and slightly heterodox author, the celebrity monk, the ecumenical mystic. He had a cottage of his own in the woods, "the Hermitage," away from the monastery's main house. He drank bourbon. He fell in love with a student nurse whom he met in a Louisville hospital while recuperating from a back operation. He died when in Bangkok for an interfaith conference: He stepped out of his bath and was electrocuted by an electric fan.

❦

Luce was a devout Presbyterian who, curiously enough, ran his business like the pope of Rome: His New York office was the Vatican and his news bureaus around the world were like the church's far-flung dioceses. His managing editors were the College of Cardinals, and his bureau chiefs were bishops and archbishops. The writers were priests and the researchers were nuns. On matters of faith and morals, Luce was infallible.

But he exercised the prerogative rarely, and even when he did, he might not be heeded and obeyed. His will might be resisted, undermined—even, in later years, ignored. He understood that, and he complained about it in fitful, caviling memos to his editors, masterpieces of sardonic understatement and a sort of bruised self-pity: *I'm only the pope, after all. Why should anyone listen to me?*

On the other hand, he admired underlings who did not obey him—and he admired himself still more for having hired them and for the fretful forbearance with which he tolerated their independent consciences and friskiness...

Up to a point, anyway.

Time Inc. wound up functioning as a sort of oligarchy. It was an empire, all right, but the editors of the various magazines set themselves up as warlords, who had their own castles and armies and might, within limits, indulge in a certain amount of ideological roughhousing and heterodoxy—active defiance or passive aggression. ∎

CHAPTER 25

I worked at *Time* in the post-Luce years, after Hedley Donovan had taken over from Luce and, after him, Henry Grunwald. In many ways, the magazine improved. Grunwald civilized it, introduced bylines, gave the magazine a more complex voice.

Donovan was a handsome and estimable Minnesotan who was, like Luce, self-possessed and inner-directed. His successor as editor-in-chief, Grunwald, was an urbane Viennese-born Jew who had fled Hitler as a boy in the 1930s with his mother and his father, Alfred Grunwald, a light opera librettist who was famous in Vienna before the war.

Grunwald was cosmopolitan, ambitious, highly intelligent. Of all my editors at *Time* over the years, I liked him best, because of his intelligence and clarity and editorial imagination. Grunwald grasped ideas instantly. He never missed the point. He was good at the nuances. I dedicated a book of my essays to him.

He had a European's tragic sense and a survivor's tragic sense and an immigrant's gratitude and avidity: He was a kind of convert to America—a little more fervent and focused than the native-born. He did not have Luce's or Donovan's sense of proprietorship about America, their certainty (as WASPs of the ruling class) about, in effect, owning the country. Grunwald was comparatively short where they were tall; he wore thick glasses; he had, shall we say, an intellectual's physique, where they had the look of broad-shouldered and lean and well-muscled former athletes. Luce graduated from Yale. Donovan went to the University of Minnesota. Grunwald worked his way through NYU. Grunwald spoke with the remnants of an Austrian accent—and with a cultivation of address that resonated with his European background. He loved opera. Luce and Donovan spoke in accents entirely American. Their speech slipped easily into a style of Thoughtful Rotarian. Grunwald would never be quite at home talking to the Rotary Club of Wichita.

In his 1997 memoir, *One Man's America*, Grunwald told the story of his privileged Vienna childhood and of his family's flight from Hitler. With the Anschluss in 1938, they abandoned their opulent apartment near the Ringstrasse and made their way to Prague, thence to Paris, where they lived for two years as refugees, scraping by on royalties that Alfred Grunwald's merry librettos (including that of his most famous operetta, *Countess Maritza*, which one critic described as counterrevolution set to music) had accumulated in countries outside Germany. Wrote Grunwald: "I learned how to be a refugee." An Englishwoman tutored him in English, using *Gone With the Wind* as their textbook.

As the Germans closed in on Paris in the spring of 1940, the Grunwalds fled again. "On the evening of May 10, a friend, the son of a well-known Viennese composer and collaborator of my father's, phoned as we were at dinner in our Paris apartment to say that he and his wife were getting out of the city, by car. Would we like to come along? Without preparation, without even much discussion, my parents and I got up from dinner, left the dishes on the table, left everything else except for a couple of small bags (and my typewriter and a part of my stamp collection, which I insisted on taking along). Then we walked out of the apartment. We piled into our friend's car, a small Peugeot, and headed south, away from the German armies."

Refugees flooded the highways. At a roadblock, an elderly policeman questioned their papers. "There ensued a bizarre scene as my father and his friend, standing on a war-choked highway with the smell of panic in the air, began crooning one of my father's songs—a waltz—in order somehow to anchor our identity in the international community of art. '*Ah*,' said the policeman after a few bars, '*je me souviens qu'on aimait danser a cette musique-là*' ('I remember we used to like to dance to that tune'). He waved them through with a smile."

After five days and nights—sleeping in barns and fields—they arrived at Biarritz. They found a child's printing press in a toy store and forged a Portuguese visa, then bribed their way onto a freighter bound for Morocco, and in Casablanca (Grunwald said the city was far less glamorous than the movie would make it out to be) eventually managed to obtain a transit visa to America. "We reached Lisbon and there managed to get a booking on the USS *Exeter*," sailing in mid-September to New York.

Grunwald loved America and adopted it as it had adopted him; he took energy from it and blessed it as his refuge and salvation from the narrowly escaped evil that killed six million Jews.

Grunwald's father never succeeded in becoming an American; he could not write his lyrics in English, so he subsided into a half-life of memories of his success in Vienna before the Nazis. But Henry, young and brash, full of energy and ideas, worked as a copyboy at *Time* to help to pay his college bills and was so bold and bright that, as the legend afterward had it, he would, as a copyboy, edit the stories he was carrying from one desk to another—so improving them that *Time* would make him, at the precocious age of twenty-eight, a senior editor.

Henry Grunwald was something of an exotic among the WASPs at *Time*. His ascent was evidence of *Time* having, in a sense, acquired a dimension of culture that it did not possess before, not in the same way. To Grunwald his success at *Time* was evidence of his arrival as an American. (He would complete the circle of his journey by returning to Vienna during the 1980s as the American ambassador to Austria, appointed by Ronald Reagan—a different sort of arrival but as satisfying as Clare Luce's when she became US ambassador to Rome under Eisenhower.) At the same time, Grunwald's success at Time Inc. signaled the company's arrival at a higher plane of cosmopolitanism and political subtlety: Grunwald was relatively conservative, but he was less categorical and, one might say, more civilized than Luce. ∎

CHAPTER 26

It was October 1964. Mary Pinchot Meyer's murder was my initiation into certain mysteries of storytelling, and into the follies of conspiracy theories and the truth that sometimes you can never know the truth. The story would haunt me. It followed me from my days as a young reporter at the *Star* and across the years. I kept a file on the case and added to it from time to time—clippings, links, notebooks—until at last, the conspiracy theories grew too outlandish and, reading them, I began to feel unclean. I gave up the small obsession.

I suppose I was half in love with Mary. Ghost love—a fascination entertained for a moment in some entirely private room of the mind. In life, men fell in love with her readily enough. Some thought that John Kennedy, who never fell in love with his women, was nonetheless in love with Mary Pinchot Meyer and that, after he had completed his second term as president, he might have divorced Jackie and married her. They might have lived happily ever after.

Except that he was dead. Except that she was dead.

I thought of Henry Kissinger's answer when some clever person asked him how he thought the course of history might have been altered if, in November 1963, it had been Nikita Khrushchev who was assassinated, rather than John Kennedy. Kissinger replied, "I am certain that Aristotle Onassis would not have married Nina Khrushchev."

❧

The murder occurred on October 12, 1964, around noon, on the towpath of the C&O Canal, just below Georgetown University. I did not know who the victim was. I rushed to the scene from the press room at police headquarters.

I knew nothing about the woman or who had shot her. The killer was off in the woods somewhere. I was certain at least that she was dead. Her body had the absolute stillness—the unmistakable fact of death.

But she had just died, and the body must still be warm. That thought occurred to me for some reason—that the body would still be warm.

I was young and had not seen many dead bodies. This was my second or third. The others had been lying in open caskets in funeral homes.

The woman was curled on her side, in the fetal position on the threadbare grass of the canal towpath in a pure, clear October sunlight. It was noontime. The trees in the woods sloping down to the river had lost half of their leaves. The remnant leaves were bright red and orange. I could not see the bullet holes. I saw no blood. The woman looked peaceful, I might have said.

She wore an angora sweater—pink or blue (I am color-blind)—and pedal pushers and what looked like ballet slippers or sneakers. I can't quite remember which. Her face was turned somewhat away from me, three-quarters of her profile hidden, yet I saw that she was lovely, or—my mind made the fine distinction—that she *had* been lovely a little earlier in her life, and that her haircut was an expensive one, blondish light-brown hair cut fairly short, with faint golden highlights toward the tips.

The moment had an eerie clarity. I stood over her body on the towpath of the old C&O Canal, which runs parallel to the Potomac. Washington, where I grew up, is sweetest just at that moment, in early fall, or else in April, when the dogwood and cherry blossoms and apple blossoms are out. Washington is famous, of course, for its trees and its southern spring.

I'd played here along the canal as a boy. My family lived in Georgetown, just up the way, on N Street. My brother and I hunted butterflies along the towpath—monarchs and swallowtails and red admirals. We caught them in a butterfly net and my brother put them in his smelly killing jar, and we watched as their wings beat more slowly and weakly until they grew still. The canal had always been squalid—brown and muddy, littered here and there with floating garbage.

There was no one on the towpath now—except for me and, of course, the body. I felt an odd sort of social discomfort. I had the half thought (I was not thinking clearly but merely taking things in, my mind working like a primitive camera—the newspaper reporter as a sort of Brownie camera) that the woman, especially as she was so newly dead, was entitled to privacy—and that my standing over her like this was bad manners. I was standing too close to her calamity, her…embarrassment. Did she mind? There was no one to see. I felt that I ought to do something, but there was nothing to do. I had arrived too late to help her—or to interview her about what had happened. What had happened was not clear. She was dead on the ground at my feet.

The police were far away down the towpath, barely visible in the distance, in blue lines, way, way to the west, in the direction of Chain Bridge, and in the opposite direction, toward Key Bridge. They had organized a dragnet to search for the killer, who was still at large. In their haste, they had left the body all alone.

In the coming years, as the hard, verifiable facts of her death receded and the myth of it emerged in a bloom and tangle of conjecture, people would try harder and harder to penetrate her privacy. They were looking for a secret—*the* secret. Journalists and conspiracy theorists always have an idea that there is a Rosebud. Often there is none.

But Mary Pinchot Meyer remained a somewhat mysterious woman. Journalists and historians and dogged paranoids could not get beyond a certain point, not after they established the tabloid basics of the narrative: that she had been one of John Kennedy's lovers and that she had visited him frequently in the White House when Jackie was away; and that her ex-husband, Cord Meyer, had worked high up in the CIA and was a mysterious and interesting man in his own right (he had lost an eye to a Japanese grenade on Guam—his twin brother Quentin died on Okinawa—and come home a war hero and founded the World Federalists but in a few years suddenly reversed course and vanished into the CIA, recruited by Allen Dulles); and that she was the daughter of Amos Pinchot (a prominent New York Progressive lawyer) and the niece of Gifford Pinchot (Theodore Roosevelt's great conservationist head of the US Forest Service) and the sister-in-law of Benjamin Bradlee (then the

Washington bureau chief of *Newsweek*, later a legend at the *Washington Post*, especially because of Watergate); and that she moved discreetly in the highest circles (social, political) but lived a genteel bohemian sort of life—a serious abstract expressionist painter of a certain talent, the lover for a time of the semi-famous artist Kenneth Noland. She was a some-time dabbler in LSD, in which pursuit she was supplied and mentored, it seemed, by Timothy Leary himself.

All these facts came out, piecemeal, as the years passed. The favorite conspiracy theory was that someone in the CIA had killed her, perhaps because she knew too much about her lover Jack's assassination.

At the time of her murder—October 1964—I was a twenty-five-year-old reporter for the *Evening Star*.

I was the first reporter on the scene—no others would arrive for quite a while. I parked my car on Canal Road, on the opposite side of the canal, and ran under the canal through an old tunnel of which I was aware from when I was a kid. Everything was somewhat wilder and overgrown then; for example, there was no causeway over to Roosevelt Island, which lay just east of Key Bridge and was as deserted as the island in the Mississippi River where Huck Finn and Jim took refuge. My brother and I would rent canoes at Fletcher's Boathouse and paddle over to explore the island. Once we found a black man drunk in the woods, asleep—we thought he was dead. He lay on his back, his mouth wide open, an empty pint bottle of Four Roses lying beside his left ear. We could not figure out how he'd gotten over to the island. He surely did not swim. He was not the type to rent a canoe.

At length, the police arrived—detectives whom I knew from the homicide squad downtown. They shooed me away from my post beside the body (about which I found I had grown as wary and protective as a dog). I retreated ten yards. The cops did not look me in the eye. Cops usually dismiss reporters as a lesser breed, almost invisible; yet quite apart from that reflex, I saw that they were embarrassed that I had been there on the murder scene for so long, by myself. They knew that I knew, perfectly well, that they had left a murder scene unsecured.

When I thought of it later, it seemed odd that the police did not overcome their embarrassment and question me about the long minutes that I spent alone with the body. They never asked me if I had seen anyone or anything. For all they knew, I might have tampered with evidence, or I might have tried to move the body. I might have planted a gun, or attempted to revive the victim, or seeded the scene with false evidence.

The police did not ask me how long I had been standing there. I might have been the killer myself, returned to the scene of the crime.

Above all, there was this: They did not ask me how I had happened to arrive at the murder scene without encountering police; they thought they had sealed off all approaches, and they firmly insisted on that in the years to come.

It occurred to me (1) that they did not even know about the hidden tunnel that I had used to come under the canal to get to the body, and (2) that if I had used that hidden tunnel, then the killer might also have used it—to escape.

So the very first moments after Mary Pinchot Meyer died introduced a world of mysteries and possibilities that would never be addressed—not in the immediate police investigation and not in the murder trial months later.

∾

Now the police pushed me aside and got things under control at last. The medical examiner's people, with big square black suitcases, began fussing over the body, doing their forensic work. Plainclothes police, all of them men in raincoats, stood in a ring around the victim, speaking in low tones. Other reporters began to arrive.

No one would know, for some hours, who the dead woman was. *Jane Doe.*

The suspect was still in the woods. They were looking for a "Negro male, five feet eight, 185 pounds, dressed in dark trousers and a tan jacket." That was the description the witness named Henry Wiggins gave. He was a gas station mechanic and he and another mechanic had been fixing a car on the other side of Canal Road when they heard a couple of shots and a scream and rushed over to a retaining wall above the canal to see a black man struggling with a white woman who was clinging to a thin sapling beside the water.

After a time, the police found Ray Crump and brought him to the towpath.

He looked at the body, and he asked the cops, "You think I done *that*?"

He was a small man, a twenty-four-year-old day laborer from Anacostia, on the opposite side of the city, whom the police arrested as he walked along abandoned trolley tracks that run through the scrubby woods between the Potomac and the canal. He was smaller than Wiggins had said—shorter by several inches and lighter by some forty pounds. His clothes were soaking wet. He claimed that he had been fishing from a rock on the riverbank and had dozed off and fallen into the water.

The trouble with that story was that his fishing pole, on that day, was standing in a closet in his apartment back in Anacostia.

The police showed Crump to Henry Wiggins, the mechanic I had talked to, and Wiggins said, "That's him!"

The police took Ray Crump to headquarters and booked him for murder.

∾

I went to a pay phone on Canal Road, not far from Key Bridge, and phoned in my notes to a rewrite man at the *Star*. We were on deadline for the City Final edition. They would remake the front page.

The medical examiner's people zipped the body in a bag and drove it to the morgue. Her death passed over into the realm of bureaucracy. She became a case, a file.

When it emerged that the victim was named Mary Pinchot Meyer and that she lived in Georgetown, in a house on 34th Street, the police tracked down her brother-in-law, Benjamin Bradlee, husband of the dead woman's sister Antoinette (Toni) Bradlee. Ben Bradlee went to the morgue to identify the body. He was accompanied on the errand by Harry Dalinsky—"Doc" Dalinsky, the pharmacist who ran the Georgetown Pharmacy at Wisconsin Avenue and O Street.

I was startled when I heard about Dalinsky. Georgetown was a small town. Bradlee lived on the same block of N Street that my family did when I was growing up. Dalinsky was a friend of my parents (as well as of practically everyone else in Georgetown). He used to supply the ammoniated Cokes that my mother sent me to fetch when I was a boy and she was sitting upright in bed on a Sunday writing her syndicated column and needed a hangover cure. Doc Dalinsky did an illegal Fourth of July fireworks business out of his pharmacy, and he stored the fireworks in our garage behind the house on N Street; if someone had dropped a match in our garage sometime around the first of July, we might have blown up all of Georgetown west of Wisconsin Avenue.

The murder lent itself, from the start, to the most extravagant speculation. In the decades that followed, the story evolved as a strange, slow-motion murder mystery: a Washington *Rashomon*. The gun was never found. Divers in wet suits searched the bottom of the canal, the Potomac. Nothing. No one could discern a motive for the killing. The case would remain unsolved, and anything was possible. No theory was too improbable.

There were a thousand questions to be asked. A man named Peter Janney, son of a CIA figure named Wistar Janney, had been a boyhood friend of Michael Meyer, the son of Mary Pinchot Meyer and Cord Meyer, when they all lived in McLean, Virginia, not so far from CIA headquarters at Langley. One evening in 1954 as Michael was walking home from watching television with his friend Peter, he was crossing Georgetown Pike, a winding, treacherous road, and a car hit and killed him. Peter Janney developed a lifelong obsession with Michael's mother Mary and in 2012 published *Mary's Mosaic*, a book in which he alleged that Mary was killed by people in the CIA—and with his own father's knowledge and complicity.

I think that Ray Crump murdered Mary Pinchot Meyer. There are mysteries, still, surrounding the case. But I was there, moments after she died, and Occam's razor tells me Crump did it.

I reason that no professional assassin would have tried to pull off a hit in broad daylight on the canal towpath, where the lines of sight from up and down the path and from across the canal, on Canal Road, were long and unobstructed. Why would a killer have attempted the sort of Mission Impossible scenario that Peter Janney invented in order to try to explain how his perfidious father and his Agency pals, monsters all, contrived to murder the beautiful Mary? Why not arrange to do it at three in the morning in her bedroom—making it look like the work of a burglar?

Ray Crump was a mentally troubled young man from a nice family that was baffled and embarrassed by him. He set fire to his girlfriend's apartment while she and their two children were in it. He was once charged with raping a thirteen-year-old girl. He was not the harmless little guy—the victim—that his defense attorney, the redoubtable Dovey Roundtree, made him out to be.

We will probably never know the truth about Mary's killer—not for certain. The conspiracy theories imply a deep, even diabolical logic; there had to be a reason she was killed—and, given her connections to the president and the CIA, it must have been a historically significant reason: She knew too much about something. To let her live would be too dangerous to powerful men.

Perhaps. But most murders are not so elaborate or so momentous in their motivation. A killer may act on an impulse, in a daze (as when, in the novel *The Stranger*, Camus's Meursault, a little blinded by the sun, killed the Arab on the beach) or in a rage; and the death comes almost by accident. There's usually no conspiracy at work except for the operation of chance; and there's frequently no motive at all, or one so trivial as to be disappointing or bathetic. A person may obey an animal reflex—a twitch of the reptilian brain. He may see a bright, shiny object. He may act in a flare of unaccountable anger or desire.

Conspiracy theories assume a craftiness and reasoned intelligence and intentionality that are rarely evident in human behavior, which is so often merely a mess. Ray Crump's life was a mess, although of course that didn't make him the murderer. Even so, if I had been on the jury, I would have voted to acquit: They never found the gun. There was no evident motive. Two eyewitnesses were on the other side of the canal, a little too far away to be absolutely certain about the man they saw on the towpath. So there was reasonable doubt—which does not necessarily mean the man was innocent.

I think that Ray Crump killed Mary Pinchot Meyer. ∎

CHAPTER 27

I found early versions of Henry Luce in the histories of his American ancestors, the Luces and the Roots and the Middletons, and in the diaries of nineteenth-century China missionaries.

I imagined Luce from letters he wrote to Lila Hotz when he was a young man in the early 1920s, just out of Yale. He had no money, being a missionary's son, and she was a willowy, chattering, brown-haired young woman from a wealthy Chicago family. Her handwriting was tall and spidery and fey, and she drew fanciful cartoons in the margins of her letters—of castles, sometimes, and of herself as a princess. She played bridge and toured Europe with her mother. Harry and Lila addressed one another as "darlingest." They called themselves "lad" and "lassie." She ended one letter, "Please tiss me dood-night."

They were married in 1923, the year the events of *The Great Gatsby* occurred. It was the year that Luce started *Time: The Weekly Newsmagazine* with Briton Hadden. Lila referred to the magazine as "your darling paper." She sounded like Daisy Buchanan.

ও

A family story said that as a little boy Harry Luce saw a stained-glass window in a church, whereon was written Christ's metaphor (or so the story claimed): "I am the root and ye are the vines..." To which little Harry, mindful of his mother's maiden name, Root, was said to have exclaimed: "I didn't know we were related to God." (What Christ said, in John 15:1–8, King James Version, was "I am the vine and ye are the branches." In Revelation 22:16, he said, "I am the root and the offspring of David.")

The story was true, in any case, to something in Luce's character—a grandiose literal-mindedness of expectation; not a sense of entitlement (no Calvinist would claim he was entitled to salvation) but rather a spacious, even cosmic awareness of the drama, the high stakes, the intimate dimension of the Absolute—the blood relationship of Self to God. In his *Education*, Henry Adams wrote that when he was a child, he naturally assumed (because of his grandfather John Quincy Adams and great-grandfather John Adams) that every family had at least one president in it.

To the child Harry Luce, God was the equivalent of Adams's presidential forebears. Luce wanted to be president himself for a time, and he tried to figure out how he might overcome the constitutional impediment: He was born outside the United States. His solution was to say that in 1898, his parents had immediately registered his birth with the American consul—and somehow that made it all right.

He never put the question to a test. His presidential ambitions had other serious problems. He would have been a terrible candidate. He did not speak well in public, having stuttered when young. He did not have an easy public manner or a talent for small talk. He was accustomed to being an autocrat, running his own empire; he was used to deference.

It also dawned on Luce that a president's time in office was limited. The Twenty-Second Amendment (proposed in 1947 after Franklin Roosevelt had been elected president four times—the last time in 1944 when he was mortally ill—and finally made law in 1951) restricted any president to two terms. A president was a comparative transient. Luce by then had been in office at Time Inc. for twenty-eight years—the length of seven presidential terms. Over so many years, his influence upon the American people and the world as editor-in-chief had become enormous.

Mussolini began as a journalist. Warren G. Harding published a paper in Marion, Ohio. Trotsky made a living for years in journalism, and so did Karl Marx. John Kennedy was so briefly a journalist (covering the founding of the United Nations) that that probably didn't count. Al Gore worked for the *Nashville Tennessean* when he was young. Walt Whitman, mystic of the American ego, author of the greatest American poem, began as a journalist. ∎

CHAPTER 28

I was interested in Otto Friedrich as a sort of anti-Luce. He was a man of many gifts and extraordinary intellectual range. He was managing editor of the *Saturday Evening Post*—once the country's leading magazine—at the time it ceased regular publication in 1969. Otto wrote an exhaustive, bitter account of the magazine's demise called *Decline and Fall*. Pretty soon, with heavy family obligations and bills to pay, he sought refuge at *Time*. He more or less hated the magazine (you saw the hatred even in his body English as he walked the corridors, close to the walls—with an almost Dostoevskian furtiveness, as if he planned to set off a bomb); and yet he worked there for many years as an editor and writer, like (as Otto thought) a concert pianist who supported his family by performing in a whorehouse.

In the preface to a collection of his articles called *The Grave of Alice B. Toklas*, Otto summarized his career. He wrote that all the pieces he had assembled in that wonderful collection were

reports from the past, that ever-expanding territory in which all choices have already been made, all actions taken, a territory now a field for reflection, for remembering or forgetting what cannot be changed. This applies just as well to my own past as to that of the human race. When one is young, one speeds nervously along in a kind of perpetual present, but as one gets older, one acquires a clearer view of the shapes of what has already evolved. In some of these stories, I am the main character, in some a minor one, in some a mere shadow in the background. Still, I write about Scarlatti because I love to play his music, and about Monte Cassino because the sight of it moved me. You can hardly avoid guessing that one of my great-grandfathers was a German judge, but another one was an officer in a New York artillery regiment that fought with Grant at Spotsylvania and the Wilderness. Their lives are also mine.

Though I have written several works of history...I am not a historian, at least not in the academic sense. I am a storyteller...I dislike the whole apparatus of "scholarship," the footnotes and the waspish euphemisms and the perpetual caution. I have worked most of my life as a journalist for institutions as different as *Stars and Stripes* and *The Saturday Evening Post*, the *New York Daily News* and *Time*, but I think that history, journalism, and autobiography are all part of the same process of storytelling, of revelation and self-revelation, of bearing witness. It is the process of the Ancient Mariner clutching at the wedding guest and insisting on his story. "There was a ship," quoth he.

Otto concluded the preface by noting that almost any of his pieces in the collection could have been a book in itself. "But the best stories almost tell themselves, at a length of their own choosing, and that length is apt to be modest."

Otto wrote more than fourteen books—on Berlin during the 1920s; on Hollywood in the 1940s; on Clover Adams, Henry Adams's wife, who killed herself; on growing roses, as Otto attempted to do; on the pianist Glenn Gould; on Manet; on losing his mind (as he thought he had at one time); on Auschwitz; on the history of the idea of the end of the world; on other subjects. He lived with his wife, Priscilla Boughton, and his five children in Locust Valley, Long Island, out among rich lawyers and investment bankers, among whom he was a bit of an oddity. Otto rode into town on the Long Island Railroad, carrying his lunch in a brown paper bag. He used the time to read. He was formidably well read. He worked at *Time* in a small cell of an office, completely bare, on the twenty-fourth floor, writing articles for the magazine; around 5:00 he left the Time-Life Building and boarded the train at Penn Station back to Locust Valley, where he sat down to his evening's work on one of his books. He was ferociously productive. His shoes were sometimes worn down at the heels. He had a professorial air of self-neglect (his teeth needed cleaning)—and yet, great pride, almost arrogance.

❧

One of Otto's employees at the *Saturday Evening Post* was Leila Luce, who worked at one point for him as a cartoon editor. She was uncharitable about him: "I worked for a man with green teeth." (In *The Grave of Alice B. Toklas*, Otto wrote, "I have always hated going to the dentist and one of the first fruits of my being old enough to leave home was that I stopped going.") Leila was the third wife of Henry Luce III (Hank), Luce the publisher's elder son, and was a close friend of mine for years.

She was once a well-known beauty, and the romantic entanglements of her youth were remarkable—with Marlon Brando, with S.J. Perelman, with J.D. Salinger, with the cartoonist Al Capp and others.

Leila had had a fling with Hank Luce when they were young and then reconnected with him in later life and married him. Hank was a difficult man, to put it mildly: an ordeal. He drank. He reminded me of my favorite joke from Leo Rosten's *Joys of Yiddish*.

I paraphrase:

Sophie and Sadie, old friends, meet by chance on Fifth Avenue. They have not seen one another in a long time.

Sadie: "Sophie, you look terrific. And look at that ring! That's the biggest diamond I've ever seen! It's the size of a golf ball!"

Sophie: "Yes, it's the Lifshitz Diamond. But unfortunately, it comes with the Lifshitz Curse."

Sadie: "The Lifshitz Curse? What's the Lifshitz Curse?"

Sophie: "Lifshitz."

Hank Luce, as it were, was Lifshitz.

❧

I did not know Otto well. I think he felt like a prisoner at *Time*; he worked there for the money. I told him once that I was considering quitting my job at the magazine in order to try freelancing. He gave me a warning look. He said, "It's cold out there."

Otto was the son of the German-born political scientist Carl Friedrich, a fervent anti-Nazi who moved permanently to the United States after Hitler rose to power; he became a professor of government at Harvard, where he taught for many years. He helped to write West Germany's constitution after the war. Otto grew up in Concord, Massachusetts, went to Harvard at a precocious age (graduating at nineteen) and immediately set off for Europe with the idea of living in Paris and becoming a great writer. He was tall, handsome, self-confident. At the Grand Hotel in Lausanne, Switzerland, he accosted the elderly Richard Strauss and asked him to look at a piano concerto Otto was trying to write. In Paris, he knocked on the door of Andre Gide, who had recently won the Nobel Prize. He invited himself to tea with the humorist Max Beerbohm in London, had dinner with the noted political scientist Harold Laski, and called on the philosopher George Santayana, "reclining in his pajamas on his bed at the Convent of the Blue Nuns in Rome." I assume he had letters of introduction from his father for at least some of these encounters.

And, in Paris, he called on Alice B. Toklas out of the blue (Gertrude Stein was dead by this time) and she befriended him and encouraged his work as a novelist. He went often to the apartment at 5, rue Christine. Toklas interrogated him kindly. He told her that he planned to complete a cycle of four novels before his twenty-first birthday. She read some of the first volume and said, "You're good, you know."

James Baldwin (Jimmy), also penniless and trying to write, became a close friend. They lived *la vie bohème* on the Left Bank.

Otto married another aspiring writer on the Left Bank, an American named Priscilla Boughton. Both were only twenty-one years old.

The writing of fiction did not flourish. Obligations closed in.

Finally, he said, "I borrowed a hundred dollars from reluctant friends, and, without saying goodbye to anyone, without taking more than one suitcase and a typewriter, fled with Priscilla to look for some kind of work in Germany."

We found a cheap hotel room in Frankfurt, overlooking a heap of rubble, and settled down to living on a daily ration of ten cigarettes and two meals of bread, cheese, and tomatoes...After about two weeks of increasing hunger and fear, I finally found a job...so lowly that I was not "authorized" to have a wife, and so we had to find shelter in one room of a German widow's house, and I commuted to work on a bicycle through the cobblestoned streets of a heavily bombed town called Darmstadt. Only then could I write to Miss Toklas and tell her what had become of me. For sixty dollars a week, I was now a copy editor on the sports desk of *The Stars and Stripes*.

She wrote back, saying she was relieved that he and Priscilla were all right; and presently someone showed Otto an essay that Toklas had written recently for the *New York Times* Sunday book section (apparently the first thing she had ever written for publication), entitled "They Came to Paris to Write." She gossiped about Sherwood Anderson and Scott Fitzgerald, about Pound and Eliot, and then came to the younger generation: "There are the G.I.s with their Bill of Rights and their second novel on the way...And there are the more serious Fulbright scholars who are writing tomes for their doctorate. There is a young, very young man named Otto Friedrich who is now working on his fourth novel and who may easily become the important young man of the future."

And yet Otto's writing stalled, and nothing seemed to work. "Everything I wrote now was bad...Something had gone wrong in Paris, in that brief three-month period when the great golden daydream was evaporating before my eyes. Through a failure of nerve, or simply a sense of survival, I had all too quickly come to realise that I wasn't going to make it...It is jarring to fail, suddenly and badly."

Poor Otto had descended from literature to sports journalism: "I was being paid to write headlines that said things like 'Phils Nip Cubs, 2-0.'"

Priscilla became pregnant and presently their first child was born, a girl, Liesel.

After a year and a half at *Stars and Stripes*, Otto took a job with United Press in London for $75 a week.

The UP was a strange but interesting place, where you were judged primarily on whether you got the news out one minute ahead of the AP or one minute later. Shortly after I got to London, King George VI died and the new Queen Elizabeth flew back from a hunting expedition in Kenya, and there was a coronation, and our man wrote a complete description of the event before it happened, all marked "hold for release." As far as I know, nobody who actually saw the coronation contributed anything whatever to the stories that described the event in vivid detail.

Otto's first novel appeared, called *The Poor in Spirit*. A reviewer in the *New York Times* remarked, "In writing about nothingness, the author unfortunately suggests having nothing to write about. The nothing he chooses is Berlin, 1947." The book earned $95.94. Fewer than 300 copies were sold. Otto never looked at the book again. "The only one who refused to be dismayed at my failure was Miss Toklas."

It was a motif, was it not? Yeats's "lad that had a sound fly-fisher's wrist" subsided into mere, disreputable journalism—journalism being seen as a fall from grace, the death of promise.

Otto, recently bright-eyed and bold, got an education, by and by, in the side of journalism that Evelyn Waugh had satirized in *Scoop*.

He was transferred to the Paris bureau of UP and some years later, in 1959, wrote an article in the *Yale Review* called "How to Be a War Correspondent." The piece was about bogus war news (Waugh's theme). During the Korean War, Otto claimed, "one curious editor eventually printed the same story and the same headline—YANKS SHELL/REDS ON HILL—for about a fortnight without attracting a single complaint from his readers."

Now the Korean War was over, and the journalistic appetite for war news shifted, *faute de mieux*, to the French and their travails in Indochina. Since Agence France-Presse relayed French army communiqués to Paris soon after they were issued in Hanoi—and since French army communiqués were almost the sole source of information about the war unless one went to the expense of maintaining a correspondent in Indochina, it made sense for UP's Paris bureau to handle the war news, perhaps putting a Hanoi dateline on the article and using the name of an ill-paid stringer as byline. At first, Otto, working in Paris, began his war articles dully enough. "I had worked on old-fashioned newspapers, where city editors were fussy about what they called 'facts.'" His opener might be something as uninspired as "The French High Command announced today."

The assistant bureau chief took Otto aside and chastised him for his "all-the-news-that's-fit-to-print" approach. What the story needed was "enthusiasm." What was enthusiasm?

Otto's analysis of it is worth quoting:

> [Enthusiasm] consists of writing about something as though it were exciting, even though you know nothing about it, even though you are thousands of miles away, even though it is not exciting at all. The basic technique involves verbs of action, lots of adjectives, a sure grasp of cliches, and a readiness to fill in gaps where the facts are missing. Next to our desk, the AFP ticker announces, for example, that "*des avions ont bombardé les communistes.*" We are not told how many planes, what type, what they dropped, or even where, but enthusiasm translates this into "Waves of American-built Bearcat fighter-bombers zoomed low over cleverly camouflaged Red positions and rained down bombs and fiery napalm..." To the enthusiastic war correspondent, Foreign Legionnaires are never just legion-naires; they are "tough" or "crack." Enthusiastic soldiers never "go" anywhere; they "slog through waist-deep rice paddies," they "wade through turbulent flood-swollen streams," or they "knife through sweltering jungles." If it is an amphibious attack, they "splash ashore in full battle kit" in a "bold, three-way land-sea-air attack."

This is pure Waugh, of course. When I read it, I thought of the lead that my friend Bob Jones (Robert F. Jones, associate editor of *Time*) had fastened upon the magazine's cover story about the air war in Vietnam, in the issue of Friday, April 3, 1965:

> Streaking in like vengeful lightning bolts, the F-105 Thunderchiefs loosed their bombs, rockets and cannon fire on a North Viet Nam highway bridge, sent it crashing into a gorge. Speeding

southeastward, they knocked out another bridge leading to Laos
and long used by the Communists to send troops and supplies
into South Viet Nam. With fuel and ordnance still to spare, the
Thunderchiefs swung back north, destroyed a key railroad bridge in
North Viet Nam. Only then did the pilots of the U.S. Air Force's
67th ("Fighting Cock") Tactical Fighter Squadron follow their leader,
Lieut. Colonel James Robinson Risner, back to their base at Danang.

Such densely overstimulated vividness had been a besetting sin of *Time*
magazine ever since its founding.

Jones, a writer in the magazine's World section, was a fairly vivid
character himself. He had fought in the Korean War. Once when we were
having a drink downstairs in the Time-Life Building, at La Fonda del Sol,
I asked him casually where he grew up.

"Korea," he said grimly, with a face full of meaning.

On that day at La Fonda, we had several drinks, and when we
emerged into the sunlight on West 50th Street, Bob started for an empty
taxi, but another man rushed ahead of him and claimed the cab himself.
Bob looked at me darkly and said, "If I had my Luger..."

Bob lived in northern Westchester County and was a hunter, of deer
and birds. Once in the *New York Times Magazine*, he wrote a bloodthirsty,
pagan, almost Nietzschean piece about the primitive pleasure of killing
with bow and arrow. The article drew a somewhat prissy rebuke from
a Manhattan psychiatrist who, in a letter to the editor, accused Bob of
barbarism or infantilism or something. The editors gave Bob an oppor-
tunity to reply, and he did that by inviting the psychiatrist to meet him
in the woods in single combat, both of them naked and armed with bow
and arrow, in a fight to the death. We will see, wrote Bob, which of us
emerges from the forest alive.

ᘓᕽ

In 1964, Otto Friedrich wrote a piece for *Harper's* that became famous and
much admired among newsmagazine writers and editors—and among
those other journalists who abhorred the newsmagazines. Otto's piece

was called "There Are 00 Trees in Russia," and it was a masterly, deadpan hatchet job on the storytelling techniques of *Time* and *Newsweek*. (The third newsmagazine, *U.S. News & World Report*, with its much smaller circulation, was let off the hook as inconsequential.) Otto, who had worked at *Newsweek* for a time, knew all the tricks.

"The average news story," he wrote,

> is a mixture of facts, background knowledge, and speculation, all carpentered into some kind of shape by the craftsmanship of a writer who knows how to create Potemkin villages...
>
> There is an essential difference between a news story, as understood by a newspaperman or a wire-service writer, and the newsmagazine story. The essential purpose of the conventional news story is to tell what happened...A newsmagazine is very different. It is written and edited to be read consecutively from beginning to end, and each of its stories is designed, following the critical theories of Edgar Allan Poe, to create one emotional effect. The news, what happened that week, may be told in the beginning, the middle, or the end, for the purpose is not to throw information at the reader but to seduce him into reading the whole story, and into accepting the dramatic (and usually political) point being made.

The artful newsmagazine story may begin with a weather lead: "The Finnish spring comes with glacial restraint. Farmhouses stand silent, ice-locked lakes mirror the stillness." Or it may start off with what Otto calls "the moving-vehicle lead": "One foggy morning in Berlin, a yellow Mercedes from the Soviet zone drew up at the tollgate at the Heerstrasse crossing point."

Or there is "the narrative opening": "The hooded gambler eyes tracked the jurors as they filed into the courtroom." (That was *Newsweek* on the trial of Roy Cohn.)

Or the "personality lead": "He roared up to his classes on his gadget-laden German motorcycle, dressed in sweat shirt, corduroy trousers, and boots." (*Newsweek* on the posthumous intellectual influence of C. Wright Mills.)

The point of Otto's piece was that the newsmagazines made a ridiculous (almost immoral) fetish of facts—the piling on of vivid, specific
details (what the candidate ate for breakfast, for example—that was a
favorite at *Time* for generations). Such details, such facts, said Otto, do
not add up to the truth but merely leave an impression of knowingness:
They are in themselves meaningless—and yet persuasive. They lend cred-
ibility, authority to the account. If *Time* in the autumn of 1936 knows
that Alf Landon (Republican candidate for president against Franklin
Roosevelt) had scrambled eggs and kidneys and oatmeal and orange
juice for his breakfast, then what does it not know—about Alf, about
everything? (It was the kidneys that made his breakfast memorable—a
reader would not forget the kidneys.)

When a newsmagazine writer did not have a particular statistic or
fact immediately available, he would write "TK" ("to kum," meaning
"to come" but written "to kum" so that the printer would know the
phrase was not part of the text) or "KOMING." If a number or stat
was missing, the writer would write "oo"—as in "There are oo trees
in Russia."

Otto said one *Time* writer recalled that problems arose when he
was doing a cover story on Egypt's President Muhammad Naguib.
He wrote that Naguib was such a modest man that his name did
not appear among the ooo people listed in *Who's Who in the Middle
East*. At another point, the writer noted that Naguib disliked luxury
and had refused to live in the royal palace, surrounded by a oo-foot-
high wall. "A cable…duly went to the Cairo stringer. There was no
answer. They changed the copy so that neither of the missing facts was
needed. Then, a week later, came a cable saying something like this:
AM IN JAIL AND ALLOWED SEND ONLY ONE CABLE SINCE
WAS ARRESTED WHILE MEASURING FIFTEENFOOT WALL
OUTSIDE FAROUK'S PALACE AND HAVE JUST FINISHED
COUNTING THIRTYEIGHT THOUSAND FIVE HUNDRED
TWENTYTWO NAMES WHOS WHO IN MIDEAST."

Otto observed that "such dedication to factual accuracy is rare, however, and it is expensive." And he tells the story of a newsmagazine editor
who wrote into a piece of copy: "There are oo trees in Russia."

The ingenious researcher assigned to the story obtained from the Soviet government the number of acres officially listed as forest; from some Washington agency she ascertained the average number of trees per acre in forests. "The result was a wholly improbable but wholly unchallengeable statistic for the number of trees in Russia."

Otto's piece had a salutary effect, I think. It caused writers and editors at the newsmagazines to be self-conscious about their own absurdities—about the mannerisms and pretensions of their storytelling. And yet, rereading the article after many years, I am struck by a certain captiousness in it—a tendency of Otto's indignation to miss the overall point. Otto was a man who could be merely fussy in his scorn and a little too contemptuous in his contempt.

Part of the overall truth of it was that Otto detested what he saw as *Time*'s—and Henry Luce's—Republican, pro-capitalist, Chamber of Commerce politics. (*Newsweek* positioned itself in the genteel center left.)

It's silly of course—and wrong—to pretend that a swarm of vivid facts and stats will add up to the truth. It's true that they may create an illusion (a Potemkin village) of truth when, in reality, the truth is something quite different.

But we come to the heart of the problem—the ways of storytelling. The truth quite often is in the details. Plutarch knew that: His unforgettable character sketches in his *Parallel Lives* over and over validate his principle that sometimes a small detail or incident may be more illuminating than the record of a great battle. It is ridiculous for journalistic hacks (like Waugh's veteran correspondent named Corker in *Scoop*) to invent garish, spurious details (and even now and then to invent a coup d'état or a revolution in Africa or Eastern Europe); and yet such abuse does not invalidate the principle of narrative specificity. Journalism is witness, and the journalist is the eye. Herodotus had an omnivorous appetite for details, for facts, even the smallest and seemingly trivial, because they added up, in his telling, to a picture of the known world. In *The Iliad*, each death in battle is unique and vivid, as is each warrior.

Is the role of the journalist fundamentally at odds with that of the storyteller? Is the journalist's obligation to seek the truth at war with the urge to tell a good story?

The courtroom answer is yes—stipulating, however, something that Herodotus understood: It doesn't pay to be dogmatic about these things. ∎

CHAPTER 29

In thinking of the ways of storytelling, consider the diarist, who is literally a journalist—keeper of a journal. The diarist is a prototype of journalism's original intent.

Some diaries touch history—or become part of literature. Samuel Pepys wrote unforgettably of the plague and the Great Fire of London in 1666. Anne Frank's diary was the testament of an innocent private life that intersected with the largest and most tragic history. Captain Robert Falcon Scott recorded what it was to die slowly in the Antarctic as he tried to return from the expedition to the South Pole. Virginia Woolf wrote her diary as reverie, as practice, because she was a writer and writing a diary was a way of keeping the instrument keen, and because, like all diarists who are artists, she savored—needed—the ongoing resonant life that she created and sustained in the flow of her thoughts on paper.

A diary is a private thing. I'm interested in the way that the public and private dimensions of a life touch one another. A great diary is one that shows an interesting personality and character as it observes an interesting world, in the round—grasping the public and private aspects of it. A great diary is one that lives—is vivid, full of life and thought and surprise.

The diaries of Henry "Chips" Channon seem to me extraordinary—for their artistry and for their interest as journalism, as inside information and running commentary, as well as endless gossip of an unusually high historical value. The American-born Channon (1897–1958) came from a Chicago family that acquired some wealth with a fleet of ships in the Great Lakes. He went to Europe as a young man, at the time of the Great War—first to France, where he had a job as honorary consul at the American embassy in Paris; an indefatigable social climber, he made amazing inroads into French high society and literary circles (lunching with Marcel Proust, with Jean Cocteau). He crossed to Oxford and London, where he embarked upon a career of still more heroic social climbing. It brought him into intimacy (sexual intimacy, in some cases) with dukes and duchesses and earls and princes and kings and queens ("royalties," as he called them). He was, to say the least, a conservative. He more or less detested the United States; he became a British citizen in 1933. He adored aristocracy, good taste, English country houses, champagne dinners, London clubs (he lost sleep over whether he would be elected to Pratt's), "bibelots," to use one of his favorite words: beautiful jewelry (he was forever sending his friends and lovers diamond and ruby studs and cuff links, pearls, or else Fabergé matchboxes, Fabergé eggs, silver cigarette cases). He was usually on the wrong side of politics and history—was a pal of Wallis Simpson and the Duke of Windsor; became a worshipper of Neville Chamberlain, detested Winston Churchill; was casually but relentlessly anti-Semitic. He married an heiress to the Guinness brewing fortune. He was bisexual—mostly ardent in the male direction. He was a member of Parliament for years and for a time served as personal parliamentary secretary to Rab Butler, Under-Secretary of Foreign Affairs in the Chamberlain government. That post at the Foreign Office, in addition to his seat in Parliament and of course his immense range of social contacts and rounds of luncheons and dinners, gave him a wealth of news items that any newspaper journalist would have envied. He had informants everywhere, and everyone lived to gossip and maneuver in the Great Game of London society and politics.

Chips failed in his two great ambitions—to gain a peerage and to achieve ministerial rank in government. Yet he was everywhere—as amusing confidant, as tireless host of dinners and luncheons that he usually described as "très réussi!" He was the friend and lover of minor European royalty (the royal families of Greece, Yugoslavia, Romania) at the time of their last undoing.

Max Hastings, the journalist and historian, described Chips Channon as "a consummate ass." That may have been true. And yet his diaries are extraordinary, both as literature and as journalism. A bowdlerized version of them was published in 1967. Recently, volumes of the full, unexpurgated versions have been coming out.

Chips was more faithful to his diary than he was to either his wife or his lovers. He wrote almost every day for years—in a vivid style, acutely observant, funny, snobbish, shrewd. His cast of characters is numerous, often famous—historic. The diaries add up to an ongoing history play. The entries covering the years from the start of World War II in Europe—when Hitler invaded Poland in September 1939—through the ousting of Chamberlain and the coming of Churchill and the time of the Blitz and the fall of Singapore and beyond are riveting. Chips is constantly exchanging hypocritical little smiles with Churchill when they meet in the corridors at the House of Commons (they dislike and mistrust each other). Chips listens to the PM's famous oratory ("we shall fight on the beaches...we shall never surrender," etc.) and admits, "He was magnificent." But Chips may have drunk a little too much champagne on the previous night with the prince regent of Yugoslavia, so he and "the P.R." are off to spend the afternoon having a Turkish bath ("a Turker") at the Royal Automobile Club and, after that, to "do some shopping" with HRH. The Duke and Duchess of Kent are forever coming to dine or having him out to Coppins for the weekend to confide secrets about the royal family. King George VI is hopeless. He should keep his mouth shut, Chips says. Chips dislikes Duff Cooper but adores his beautiful wife, Diana Cooper. And so on.

The Channon diaries qualify as journalism in interesting ways. He was an intelligent observer moving in the highest circles of British life at moments of historic crisis. Just as Samuel Pepys's account of London in its crises is invaluable, so with Channon.

Journalism normally seeks the widest possible readership. It is meant to be seen—immediately. Chips Channon kept his diary a secret from almost everyone; scarcely anyone knew he was writing one. He kept it locked up. He stipulated in his will that the diaries (a mass of writing totaling millions of words) should not be read by anyone until sixty years after his death.

For whom, then, did he write? What was the point of it?

Many who undertake to write a diary give it up soon enough—in a week, a month, six months. Chips went on for decades. But why? For the pleasure of living his life twice, as it were? Out of narcissism—the diary being the reflecting pool of Narcissus? Chips had immense self-regard yet, at the same time, a curious objectivity about himself and his limitations: He quite objectively wrote himself off as an essentially frivolous man, even though he rejoiced in being regarded, for a time, as the leader of London society.

Did he write because he sought to live deliberately, and on his own terms? Because the turning of his life into literature (and Chips knew how well he wrote) seemed to justify an otherwise fainéant existence? Because it made his life seem both real and important? Because it helped him to know what he thought—especially about himself?

I believe it was because—as a man who took immense pleasure in spectacles, and in dinner parties perfectly brought off, très réussi, and in brilliant, witty conversation, and in his bibelots, and in beautiful women and splendid young men, his "enchanting Pierrots"—the diary itself became to him a sort of grand bibelot, an aesthetic pleasure, a work of art whose value became all the greater in the world of his secret, pleasure-hoarding self, precisely because it was a secret, because the exquisite enjoyment of it was withheld from everyone except himself. The diary was a secret vice and a solemn vocation.

For all of that, the Channon diary is a living thing, as alive and observant and intelligent as the mind that produced it. And, *au fond*, it reproduces, *en effet* (precious Chips was constantly interjecting phrases in French), an era—most spectacularly, England and Europe between the wars, especially from the perspective of the upper classes: the peers and the "royalties." There is an endless flow of champagne. There is caviar, there are plovers' eggs. There is the long-running drama of Chips's marriage to Honor Guinness, a fabulously rich but impenetrably stolid (according to Chips) heiress who ends by running off with a farmer named Woodman, who is married and smells of the barnyard and teaches her all about raising pigs. Chips sends her a Christmas present: an elegantly bound edition of *Anna Karenina*.

Honor sends him a nice thank-you note; she doesn't get the joke. ■

CHAPTER 30

Or consider the *Baburnama*, the memoirs of Zahīr-ud-Dīn Muhammad Bābur (1483–1530), founder of the Mughal empire and a great-great-great-grandson of Timur.

There is the journalism in which the journalist is resident or citizen and reports whatever is news in his city or country: a murder, a fire, an election. And there is the journalism of someone like Herodotus or Bābur—travelers, explorers, passing through the country and reporting what may be new to them or their readers.

The *Baburnama* is an extraordinary work by a Timurid prince who mostly busied himself establishing his power base in Kabul and from there, launching an invasion into northwestern India and establishing the Mughal empire that his descendants would expand and rule over for three centuries.

Bābur, in the midst of his military and political labors, observes and records everything—the manners of the people, their ways. He was well read and had a talent for writing what the newsmagazines centuries later would call "bioperse"—biography and personality, character sketches. Here is his portrait of a man named Umar Shaykh Mirza, who was

> short and fat, and couldn't fasten his tunic without holding his breath; sometimes the ties popped. He was sloppy and unceremonious in dress and speech; he died by toppling into a ravine with his doves and dovecote. He was well read and literate, and he had some poetic talent. His sense of justice was great. Good-natured, talkative, eloquent, outspoken, brave and valiant, he performed deeds of valor.

He used to drink a lot. He was fun to be with at a gathering. He
played backgammon and occasionally gambled.

Bābur never fails to report on the quality of the water and the air of
a place he visits or conquers, and its fruits, which were precious to him:
figs, pears, melons, and the rest.

"In Isfara, nine leagues to the southwest of Margilan, there is running
water and pleasant gardens. Many fruit trees, most of the gardens are
almond groves... The saying goes, apples of Samarkand and pomegranates
of Khodzhent. But today, the pomegranates of Margilan are much better."

He shares local lore: "Between Khodzhent and Kanibadam is a
desert wilderness called Ha Darwesh. There, a fierce wind blows east
toward Margilan and west to Khodzhent. It is said that several dervishes
encountered the wind there and, unable to find each other, cried out,
'Hey, dervish.' Over and over until they all perished. From that time, the
place has been called Ha Darwesh."

The scholar and orientalist Stanley Lane-Poole wrote:

His Memoirs are no rough soldier's chronicle of marches and coun-
termarches... they contain the personal impressions and acute reflec-
tions of a cultivated man of the world, well read in Eastern literature,
a close and curious observer, quick in perception, a discerning judge
of persons, and a devoted lover of nature; one, moreover, who was
well able to express his thoughts and observations in clear and vigor-
ous language. The shrewd comments and lively impressions which
break in upon the narrative give Babur's reminiscences a unique and
penetrating flavor. The man's own character is so fresh and buoyant,
so free from convention and cant, so rich in hope, courage, resolve,
and at the same time so warm and friendly, so very human, that
it conquers one's admiring sympathy. The utter frankness of self-
revelation, the unconscious portraiture of all his virtues and follies,
his obvious truthfulness and a fine sense of honor, give the Memoirs
an authority which is equal to their charm. If ever there were a case
when the testimony of a single historical document, unsupported by
other evidence, should be accepted as sufficient proof, it is the case

with Babur's memoirs. No reader of this prince of autobiographers can doubt his honesty or his competence as witness and chronicler.

Witness and chronicler.

Bābur's travel journalism—for that is what much of the *Baburnama* amounted to, the travel writing of an observant and lively conqueror— reminded me, in its specificities, its details, its local color, of William Cobbett's *Rural Rides*, a record of his tours around the English country-side, written between 1821 and 1826. Cobbett was a delightfully cranky journalist, publisher, pamphleteer, and political eccentric who called himself "The Porcupine" and was distinguished by a strong contrarian streak. He opened a bookstore in Philadelphia just after the American Revolution and put a picture of King George III in the window. Like Bābur, he gave careful attention, in *Rural Rides*, to exact descriptions of the soil (even, in Cobbett's case, the composition of it, for he possessed the knowledge of a scientific farmer), the condition of farms, the crops, the fruits, how people lived. A probing and skeptical journalist, he wrote of one encounter: "I met a farmer going with porkers to Highworth market. They would weigh, he said, four score and a half, and he expected to get 7s. 6d. a score. I expect he will not. He said they had been fed on barley-meal; but I did not believe him. I put it to his honor whether whey and beans had not been their food. He looked surly, and pushed on."

But what I love about Cobbett are his obiter dicta:

On writing history: "One page at the end of each reign, telling us what men got for their work, and what they paid for their food, would have been better calculated than all the rest of the history, to make us judge correctly of the goodness or badness of the government."

On publicity: "When a man is bitten with the love of hearing himself talk, and of seeing his name in print, little short of a sledge-hammer, applied to his head, can discourage him."

On proximity to power: "There is something contagious in the touch of princes. Most men, who have been admitted to converse with them, become their eulogists...I can discover no other general cause for this than vanity, the vanity, the empty vanity, of being considered as a friend of the prince...Two countrymen being in a wood, where King William was hunting, said the one to the other in a tone of exultation, 'the King rode so close by me that he almost knocked me down.' 'Aye,' said the other, 'but he spoke to me.' 'Indeed! What did he say?' 'Why he said, with such a noble voice, Stand out of the way, you son of a b—.'" ∎

CHAPTER 31

The great banquet was held in Radio City Music Hall, just across Sixth Avenue from the Time-Life Building, on the northern edge of Rockefeller Center, on a Tuesday night toward the end of March 1998. With a burst of its former extravagance, *Time* magazine celebrated its seventy-fifth birthday: the diamond jubilee. Carpenters transformed the famous Art Deco theater—home of the Rockettes and, at the time of its opening in 1932, the largest auditorium in the world—into an immense, terraced banquet hall. They covered the 6,000 seats with floorboards and carpeting and, for the 1,200 guests, they installed tiers of round tables, each of them set with eight places.

The stars of the evening were several generations of actors, politicians, baseball players, boxers, industrialists, scientists, ballet dancers, and assorted geniuses, along with the president of the United States, Bill Clinton, and his wife.

Each of them had appeared on the cover of *Time* magazine. For much of the twentieth century, appearing on *Time*'s cover was, in a secular way, something like being beatified by the Catholic Church; to be chosen *Time*'s Man of the Year (or, after 1999, Person of the Year) was to be canonized.

The elect—all manner of heroes and a few villains and various gods and goddesses and icons and movie stars—stepped from taxis and limousines on Sixth Avenue. They pushed through the glass doors into the music hall's lobby; their eyes grew wide as they stared at this world-historical casting call. There was something sweet in the spectacle of the very famous gawking at the still more famous. Muhammad Ali shuffled over to Bill Gates and asked if they might have their picture taken together.

There was a cocktail hour in the lobby before everyone passed into the great hall for dinner. I stood talking to Elie Wiesel. Joe DiMaggio suddenly materialized. (He would be seated at dinner next to Henry Kissinger, a baseball fan.) In bounced Mickey Rooney, round and old and short. There was Mary Tyler Moore, looking dim and brittle now— her old self on the sixth carbon. Tom Hanks. Mel Brooks and his wife Anne Bancroft. John Glenn. Lee Iacocca. Matt Lauer. Jerry Falwell. Sean Connery. John Kennedy Jr. appeared, editor of his new magazine called *George*, all radiant with the future that lay ahead of him—a youth among so many apparitions from the past. Minister Louis Farrakhan of the Nation of Islam drifted past—his face smooth and imperturbable, with his air of menacing amusement. Over there, a curio: Jack Kevorkian—"Dr. Death"—the euthanasia activist who went around the country helping people kill themselves. I felt like Scrooge in *A Christmas Carol*, during his vision of Christmas Past.

ℰℐ

Elie Wiesel had never appeared on the cover of *Time*, but he had the Nobel Peace Prize (an equivalent distinction); he was invited to the party as an established moral celebrity of the twentieth century. Six years earlier, he and I and Abe Rosenthal had flown into Sarajevo to visit the civil war between the Bosnian Serbs and Bosnian Muslims—dipping a toe in the war for a day or two and then retreating to a first-class hotel in Switzerland to order room service and file a story bragging about the experience. I had felt a little ashamed of myself, as journalists do—popping in and out of people's suffering.

Time magazine organized itself from the start around the almost cynical principle of *not* being there: The stories were assembled by writers like me and by famously heavy-handed editors. Like the miller's daughter in "Rumpelstiltskin," I sat in a tower room in Rockefeller Center, surrounded by straw (a litter of clips and correspondents' files and other stray information) and struggled to turn the straw into gold by morning, when the king (here, *Time*'s managing editor) would arrive on his train from Greenwich. And so on. But who, or what, played the role of Rumpelstiltskin in this laborious metaphor?

Elie Wiesel's fame and moral authority had prepared the way to Bosnia—had gotten us seats on a windowless UN supply plane dropping into the war zone and secured audiences with the Serbian leaders Slobodan Milošević (whom we met in a dim, musty official sitting room in Belgrade before we left for Bosnia) and Radovan Karadžić (in a curiously American-looking rural schoolhouse). We, wearing flak jackets and blue helmets, reached the schoolhouse in a convoy of UN armored cars, winding up into the hills above Sarajevo. From those heights, Serbian snipers, fortified by slivovitz, fired down at all hours at people in the city below while other Serbs lobbed mortar shells in a recreational way in order to see the city of Sarajevo jump and suffer.

Now, in the lobby of the music hall, Elie and I gossiped about people we knew. At this point we were both University Professors at Boston University. He had started his career (after the war, after Buchenwald and Auschwitz) as a journalist in Paris.

Suddenly, Elie looked over my shoulder. His face grew ashen.

"My God," he said. "That's Leni Riefenstahl!"

ભ

Many of the assembled were still superstars, still in the game; many more were instantly recognizable, well preserved, and still themselves, though in a mellowing, emeritus way. But some were ancient ruins—their former glory effaced or altogether extinguished. They had collapsed back into the dimension of the anonymous and ordinary. Such wraiths stirred among the tables to stare at one another, searching each other's faces as if to catch an inkling or an ember of what they had been. Their former fame had fetched up on a far shore, at this surreal reunion.

ભ

That night in the music hall had a quality of a great durbar, or of Queen Victoria's own diamond jubilee ("On dune and headland sinks the fire" etc.) and yet also of vaudeville ("He's the man who broke the bank at Monte Carlo!"), or of Madame Tussaud's wax museum come to life—mythic figures (authentic myths, if you see what I mean) dragged into a magazine's quite handsome and lifelike publicity stunt.

Or perhaps I should say the reunion looked like a photograph of the MGM commissary in the 1930s or 1940s, when all the studio's iconic actors (many of them wearing their movie costumes as pirates or queens or famous lovers) were gathered to gossip and have lunch—and to wink at the camera as if to acknowledge that they had been caught in their imposture.

Time Inc.'s reign—and that of the print media—was in its waning days (as the British Empire was at the time of Victoria's jubilee in 1897). A new century and a new millennium were just around the corner. New technologies were about to rearrange the world.

❧

Would Hitler or Stalin have been invited to the banquet if they had still been alive? Hitler had been *Time*'s Man of the Year in 1938; Stalin in 1939 and 1942. Thousands of readers had canceled their subscriptions at the time, shocked at finding such beasts called "Man of the Year," but *Time* patiently reminded them (with a self-importance that was one of the magazine's irritating traits, a legacy of Luce) that it did not bestow the title of Man of the Year because it approved of the man, but merely to acknowledge that, in that particular year, that particular man had had more impact than anyone else upon the world and its history. If that impact had involved great evil, why, that only proved *Time*'s point.

Would their sheer historical importance have gotten Hitler and Stalin an invitation to the seventy-fifth anniversary? I wasn't sure. No less a moralist than Dante had organized an immense reunion of sinners in his *Inferno*. I knew that, in the Luce fashion, there would have been solemn discussions of the matter during editorial lunches upstairs in the private dining rooms.

If Luce had been alive to plan the seventy-fifth anniversary dinner, he might have asked his housecarls, "Can we invite Hitler without inviting Stalin? Or invite Stalin without Hitler? And what about Mao? God knows it goes against my grain, but we ought to think about it." So many issues of protocol. He would have invited his favorites, Chiang Kai-shek and the Madame, and it would have been awkward to have them along with Mao and Chou En-lai.

Rick Blaine (Humphrey Bogart) had a similar seating problem when Victor Laszlo showed up at his club in Casablanca on the same night as Major Strasser and his Nazi entourage.

ფ

Luce would have presided over a luncheon conference.

Some editors would have argued earnestly that the seventy-fifth anniversary was historic and that all the magazine's cover subjects, good or bad (or, in a few cases, evil), must be beckoned to the feast, regardless of their crimes. *Time*, as journalist-witness (but not as judge—for judging was not the purpose of the occasion), must stand a little outside the flow of history and welcome all the greats to the spectacle. This was Valhalla. The magazine for seventy-five years had recorded a comprehensive pageant, explaining it all as the world proceeded from crisis to crisis, from Jazz Age to Great Depression to Second World War to Hiroshima and Truman and Ike and Kennedy and Dallas and Vietnam and on beyond.

The banquet would amount to an immense summation and curtain call. The actors had converged to take a bow.

Put another way, they had been summoned from the corners of the earth so that *Time* itself, and the ghost of Henry Luce, might take a bow.

ფ

Other editors would have argued against inviting the monsters. They would have asked, "Do we really intend to sit down to dinner with men like Hitler and Stalin? It would be as if we had forgiven them, as if their crimes were not real. *Time* has always worked in a zone somewhat beyond journalism. We justified that by claiming to be moral in our judgments of the news. We have always claimed it was our business, our prerogative, to condemn or to forgive, after we sifted the evidence. Wouldn't it be immoral to suspend our judgment of Hitler and Stalin for the sake of—what?—spectacle? Publicity? We're getting into some sketchy areas of journalistic ethics."

There were always editors at *Time* who sounded like that—like the first mate, Starbuck, trying to persuade Captain Ahab to stick to honest whaling.

Harry Luce would have fallen into one of his impenetrable silences. His editors would have stared at their lamb chops.

&

Should *Time* invite Pol Pot to the party? He was still alive in March 1998, after all—though he had only a month to live. The party's hosts could not have known that. I liked to picture a *Time* stringer setting out from Phnom Penh carrying an engraved invitation, assigned to search out the fugitive, mass-murdering ideologue Pot in his jungle camp. RSVP.

Ho Chi Minh was long dead, but General Vo Nguyen Giap lived on and might have responded to an invitation from *Time*. No doubt, like Mikhail Gorbachev, General Giap had his vanity—and what superb vindication it might have been for him to show up at the seventy-fifth anniversary of the magazine that had pronounced the American mission against him to be "the right war in the right place at the right time."

Giap was North Vietnam's military genius who kicked the French out of Indochina in 1954, in the Battle of Dien Bien Phu, and did the same to the Americans twenty-one years later. It was Giap's face that appeared on the cover of *Time* the week after Saigon fell in April 1975 and the Americans fled, pushing their helicopters into the South China Sea.

&

President Bill Clinton was in the thick of the Monica Lewinsky scandal. He and Hillary Clinton showed up wearing expressions that were frozen in misery, embarrassment, anger—the president downcast and woebegone and his wife in what looked like a barely suppressed state of rage. So it seemed to me as I watched them. Others thought they looked chipper enough.

When the speeches were over and the hall was all but empty, President Clinton, looking like an adolescent who had just wrecked his father's Cadillac, stood alone on the Radio City Music Hall stage. No one would come near him. I saw his sometime pollster and close adviser, Dick Morris, standing off to one side of the hall, staring at the president and wrestling with strong emotions, trying to decide whether to go to Clinton (to console him? to advise him?), as he had done in former days of trouble. They had become estranged. Morris had been cast out. Now Morris—a short, squat, powerful man—worked his jaw and bit his lips in an agitation of conflicting impulses. At last, he shook his head and turned his back and shuffled toward the exit.

Mikhail Gorbachev came out of the shadows. I saw him out of the corner of my eye. He materialized like a Polaroid photograph, emerging slowly into view with the famous birthmark stain on his forehead. He arrived with his small, fastidious interpreter, the one with the mustache who had appeared at all the summit meetings with Ronald Reagan. *Time* honored Gorbachev as the "Man of the Decade" at the end of the 1980s, just as the Soviet empire disintegrated. Since then, the world had ignored him. When the time came for speeches (everyone was supposed to be brief, a few minutes, no more), Gorbachev took the Radio City stage and droned on and on and on in fussy Russian, parsing a thousand grievances about the state of the world, as his interpreter rendered the monologue into English.

Every hero becomes a bore at last, Emerson wrote. At my table, the television news anchor Peter Jennings, in a frolicsome mood, proposed that the next time Gorbachev paused, all of us should leap to our feet, applauding wildly, hoping that Gorbachev would take the hint.

ↇ

Earlier, as Elie and I talked in the lobby, Lauren Bacall slid by at an angle—her green eyes darting nervously about the room, her face lightly ravaged by the years since 1966, when she had appeared on *Time*'s cover to illustrate a story about what the magazine called "The Pleasure & Perils of Middle Age."

That *Time* story thirty-two years earlier had been a pretty fair sample of the magazine's prose and methods at the time—of its self-confident, still-Lucean manner and mannerisms: its way with statistics for example, as it labored to present the cover story's thesis in an onslaught of generalizations about what it called "the command generation":

> Without the Bacall good looks but with the selfsame vitality, other members of the command generation are the helmsmen of U.S. society in government, politics, education, religion, science, business, industry and communications. From President Johnson, 57, and Vice President Humphrey, 55, through the entire Cabinet including Rusk, 57, and McNamara, 50, the top echelon of government is middle-aged. Including that anachronistic middle-ager, Bobby Kennedy, 40, the 100 U.S. Senators tally up an average age of 57, and the House of Representatives is seven years younger at a representative 50. Sixty-three percent of this country's Nobel prizewinners in the past ten years have been between 40 and 60. At 15 of the leading U.S. colleges and universities, the average presidential age is 55; of 900 executives in 300 top corporations, only a handful falls outside the 40–60 group.

As I read the paragraph, I thought of the poor researcher who had labored to check all those stats. I believe she was Betty Suyker—a charming and enormous woman in the magazine's Show Business section. This was a perfect example of the sort of thing Otto Friedrich satirized in his article "There Are 00 Trees in Russia."

※

Steven Spielberg rose to pay tribute to John Ford. He said:

> The most famous line John Ford ever directed is this one: When the legend becomes fact, print the legend. And he believed that, believed that without legends to inspire us, we cannot be our best selves or fulfill our promise as a nation. On this occasion, as we celebrate an

institution [*Time*] that has always strived to tell us the hard truths about our times, it's good to remember that we cannot live without our bright legends either.

How to sort out the complex, intermingled truths and untruths that Spielberg packed into that paragraph? The line came from John Ford's 1962 film, *The Man Who Shot Liberty Valance*, starring John Wayne and James Stewart. It was the last time that John Ford directed John Wayne in a picture. Over the years they had made twelve movies together, including *Stagecoach*, *She Wore a Yellow Ribbon*, *Fort Apache*, *The Quiet Man*, and the extraordinary one called *The Searchers*. *Liberty Valance* was Ford's mordant farewell to the western—the genre for which he had a particular genius. (He would introduce himself, "My name's Ford. I make westerns.")

Liberty Valance and that familiar line ("print the legend") raised questions that bothered me for years about *Time*'s journalism—all journalism.

Henry Luce by some alchemy (not a very complicated alchemy, really—maybe it had merely to do with exaggeration and the artful selection of details) used his publications, especially *Time*, to create—to proliferate—legends. Legends endure. Legends are memorable. Everything vanishes into the country of myth, Thucydides said; *Time* magazine hastened the process. People become legends; Luce almost always put people on the cover of *Time*.

It was the John Wayne character, Tom Doniphon, who shot Liberty Valance (a sort of local monster, played by Lee Marvin). The James Stewart character, Ranse Stoddard—a lawyer, a dude, and eventually a successful politician, governor of the territory—was mistakenly credited with the killing. He did not correct the mistake but rather bragged about the deed and built his political career on it.

Unfairly, perhaps, I thought of Lieutenant (j.g.) John F. Kennedy on board PT-109 that night in the Blackett Strait in the Solomons—when he was careless enough to allow his boat to be sliced in two by a Japanese destroyer. He behaved heroically in the aftermath (swimming for many hours to get help for the surviving members of his crew). Both Kennedy and his crew thought of it, at the time, as an inglorious business. They were ashamed of what had happened. But as the story was told and retold and became a legend, the heroism became mainly the point of it and not the fact of the skipper's incredible sloppiness in letting his PT boat get run down by a Japanese destroyer. Two of his crew died outright.

John Hersey wrote an article in the *New Yorker* about PT-109. (He and Kennedy had known one another before; Hersey married one of Kennedy's old girlfriends.) The *New Yorker* piece was the beginning of the legend. Joe Kennedy persuaded *Reader's Digest* to print a condensed version of the tale, which thus was read by millions well beyond the orbit of the *New Yorker*. The ambassador had the article reprinted and distributed to voters during Jack's 1946 run for Congress and in political campaigns thereafter. The PT-109 story became an origin myth of that other, larger legend, Camelot.

Saul Bellow wrote, "We all need our memories. They keep the wolf of insignificance from the door." We all need our legends, for the same reason. America itself is a legend. Radio City Music Hall that night was filled with people whom *Time* had helped to turn into legends. Many of them were glorious and heroic and deserved all of *Time*'s superlatives—Jonas Salk, Mikhail Gorbachev, Joe DiMaggio. There were a lot of movie actors, too, some still handsome and beautiful, but you had to think that, with them, the matter of legends and authenticity began to be problematic, for here you entered a hall of mirrors; they had been in the legend-making business themselves. Among the actors were Mickey Rooney and Sharon Stone, Sophia Loren and Kevin Costner, Tom Cruise, Jodie Foster, and Sean Connery. There were moviemakers—Spielberg, Harvey Weinstein. There were journalists who had gotten to be mythic themselves: the big three anchormen Walter Cronkite, Dan Rather, Tom Brokaw; the *Times'* Abe Rosenthal.

The legends had aged, some of them disastrously, some well. You saw the wear and tear—the drama of their troubles: Muhammad Ali was an impressive ruin of the man he'd been. You thought, in a banal way, about the passage of time. If you summon a legend back into the realm of actual time, of the mortal self, if only for an evening, then the legend may be compromised—or anyway confused. It's as if, coming back to take a bow, they were debunking themselves.

It was as if the dinner had revised the *Liberty Valance* quote ("print the legend") and had said, instead, "If you look closely at the facts of the legend, you may be obliged, despite yourself, to acknowledge that time wins in the end and that legends become a bit of an anticlimax."

Walter Isaacson, by now managing editor of *Time*, praised Bill Clinton for the achievements of his administration. Noting the seventy-fifth anniversary, he predicted an even more glorious future for Henry Luce's iconic magazine. Walter would leave *Time* by and by and go on, in the twenty-first century, to become the best-selling biographer of geniuses: superbly intelligent books about Albert Einstein, Steve Jobs, Benjamin Franklin, Leonardo da Vinci. In doing that, he turned one of Luce's journalistic principles into his own unique formula.

That night felt like the end of something—the end of Henry Luce, anyway. There was a generational dynamic at work. Isaacson and Jim Kelly and Rick Stengel and other top editors at *Time* were baby boomers. Their accession to power at Luce's magazine had represented a change of zeitgeist there; they brought with them the baggage of their generation's experience and of the 1960s. Bill and Hillary Clinton were also boomers, and so was Donald Trump, although of course he came from a different part of the forest. They were proto-boomers, born in 1946–1947, in the first wave of that tremendous generation. With the coming of the boomers to Luce's old empire, the place became something different from what it had been. Henry Luce had been King Lear, "the old majesty." Some of the new people had the unpleasant tendencies of Goneril and Regan. They brought a certain impatient depthlessness to the work. They lacked resonance.

The American presidency (with the power of which Luce had always so closely identified himself and his magazines, as if he were a kind of shadow president) had itself been one of America's most important legends; but here on the Radio City stage stood the current president, a boomer, a very bright and dodgy and middle-aged juvenile. The seventy-fifth anniversary became, among other things, a festival of supersession; the baby boomers, for good or ill, had triumphed.

To look at it in quite a different way—as it were, through the other end of the telescope—the dinner had felt like a fiftieth college reunion.

The old grads of twentieth-century history had gathered in the music hall to inspect one another, with, shall we say, a journalistic curiosity. Everyone contemplated the assembled achievements and past glories; everyone also took note of how badly, or how well, each of them had aged.

After it was over, I walked out through the glass doors onto Sixth Avenue, and I looked up at the Time-Life Building across the way, its offices mostly dark now. I watched John Kennedy Jr. walk away briskly, heading north in the cold and rain. It occurred to me that the twentieth century had gotten old. That night, it was almost exactly one hundred years since Henry Luce had been born in a Presbyterian mission in China while, at that same moment, on the other side of the world, William Randolph Hearst's newspapers, with a fine sense of publicity and frolic, stirred up the Spanish-American War.

Selah. ■

ACKNOWLEDGMENTS

My deepest gratitude to Louise Grunwald for her generous support of my Henry Grunwald Senior Fellowship at the Ethics and Public Policy Center. The fellowship honors Louise's late husband, for whom I worked over a period of years when he was managing editor of *Time*, and later, editor-in-chief of Time Inc. He was a friend and the favorite editor of my long career in magazines and newspapers.

My thanks as well to Tom and Alice Tisch, whose support has helped me to go on writing books and articles. I'm deeply grateful to them.

Thanks to Ryan T. Anderson, president of the Ethics and Public Policy Center, and to his predecessor, Ed Whelan, for their help and many kindnesses.

Some passages in this book—notably those discussing Robert Caro and certain memories of *Time* magazine—appeared first in *City Journal*. As always, I am grateful to *CJ*'s editor, Brian Anderson, and managing editor, Paul Beston.

Finally, I am indebted to Paul Gigot and James Taranto at the *Wall Street Journal*, where I publish occasional essays.

INDEX